Winning The Wealth Game With Shares

How You Can Make Money and Become Wealthy in the Stock Market

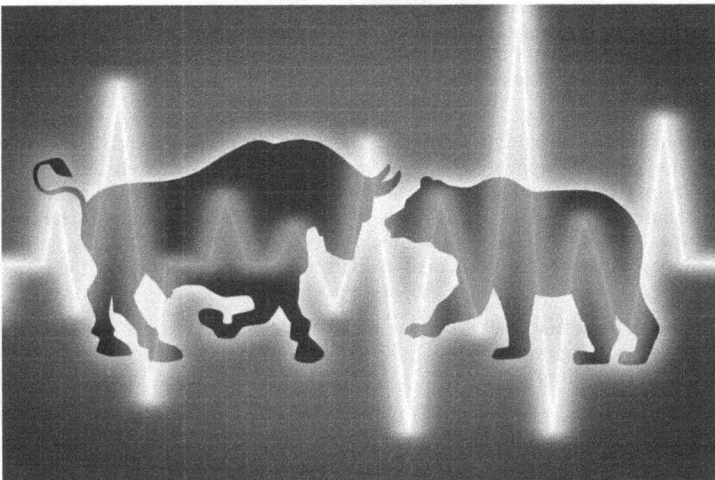

Mark Robinson, Glen Wilson and Easen Evans

Best Seller Success Publishing
Sydney, Australia
Las Vegas, Nevada, USA
+1 (702) 997 2229
+61 (02) 8005 4878

Special Offer

Would you like to find out if an automated share trading platform is the right vehicle for your situation?

Book in right now for your FREE consultation, your bonus for reading this book.

To Grab Your Bonus Session go to

http://www.winningthewealthgame.com.au/sharesbookoffer

Not all share strategies are created equal. We will share more information on how automated systems can save you time and make money. Look forward to speaking to you soon.

Table of Contents

About Mark Robinson.. ix

About Glenn Wilson.. xii

About Easen Evans.. xiv

A Note From the Authors.. xv

Winning the Wealth Game With Shares............................... 17

What are Shares?.. 21

    Background... 22

    Advantages and Disadvantages................................. 27

    Why Own Shares?.. 31

    Risks of Investing in Stock.................................. 39

    Cost of Capital and Risk..................................... 41

    The Psychology of Trading 47

    Visuals.. 60

    Money Management... 64

Types of Shares.. 71

    Ordinary Shares.. 71

    Preference Shares 71

    Commodities.. 74

    Options.. 74

About Market Sectors 80

Trends 80

Secret to Long-Term Gains 85

Sector Analysis... 90

Why Invest in Shares/Equities.. 95

The Difficulty of Diversification..................................... 99

Diversification or "Diworseification"............................ 102

Judging your Portfolio 107

Getting Started 111

What are my goals? 113

When should I start?... 115

How much should I invest? 117

How should I invest?.. 118

When should I sell? 120

Rising Markets 121

Falling Markets... 126

What to Trade... 131

Shares.. 131

Futures Contracts 135

Options 137

Positions 138

Warrants.. 142

Exchange-traded products 143

Contracts for Difference (CFD's)................................144

Real Estate Investment Trusts (REIT's)........................144

Interest rate securities 145

Credit-linked notes 145

Increasing Returns without Leverage 147

Increasing Returns with Leverage 153

Super and Shares: What's the connection?.....................157

Robotic Trading..165

Pros and Cons of Robotic Trading.............................169

Useful Links...179

Special Offer..182

Other Books in the Series....................................183

About Mark Robinson

Mark Robinson, founder and CEO of Acquire Wealth Solutions loves nothing more than helping Business Owners and Property Investors set up, grow and protect their wealth. His actions speak for themselves, creating seven successful companies in a four year period as well as a charity dedicated to a hand-up not a hand-out approach. His last company broke even in three months, became profitable in six and hit a six-figure income in nine months. His clients describe Mark as very professional and proactive with his advice.

Mark has written seven books and has been involved with property transactions for his clients worth over $365 million dollars. Mark has an ability to translate the complexities of the modern financial world into simple easy-to-understand language.

This allows his clients to grasp his recommendations with the understanding required to succeed. Mark uses a simple formula that looks at where you are today, where you want to be and then works out which steps will be the best for you to get there. Mark always works with the end in mind. What you are trying to achieve is foremost in his mind. Mark has the ability to help you take what you have learned in seminars, webinars etc, and turn that knowledge into a viable and actionable financial plan.

This means we can look at all scenarios and not be stuck with traditional thinking. We will look at property, shares, managed funds, superannuation and businesses. You see, most traditional Financial Planners will only look at managed funds because they just do not understand property or business instruments. "Why planners overlook property and businesses is beyond me," Mark states.

Mark loves helping business owners increase their profits and exposure using the latest information and technology, such as Infusionsoft, Facebook, Twitter and LinkedIn.

Personal

Mark lives in beautiful Sydney with his wife Billie and two gorgeous girls, Jasmine-Rose and Riley-Jane. He loves spending time with his family either relaxing by the pool or down at the park or beach. He also enjoys travelling and has spent time in Europe, Asia, USA, New Zealand and has been across most of Australia.

Education and Experience

Licensed Financial Planner. Diploma in Financial Services and Financial Planning. Diploma in Financial Services Mortgage Broking. Mark Robinson is an Authorized Representative, No 243170 of My Planner, and AFSL No 345905

Mark has authored and co-authored a number of books in The Wealth Game and Winning the Wealth Game series.

Titles include:

Winning the Wealth Game by Protecting Your Assets

Winning the Wealth Game in Business

Winning the Wealth Game by Creating Multiple Streams of Income

Winning the Wealth Game with Stocks

Winning the Wealth Game Using Property

Winning the Wealth Game Online

Winning the Wealth Game in Network Marketing

Helping Business Owners and Property Investors to set up, grow and protect their Wealth is his mantra.

Mark is known as Australia's leading wealth protection and creation expert. After writing *Seven Steps to Wealth Protection and Your Path to Wealth*, he has written *Winning the Wealth Game in Business*, a step-by-step guide that tells you how you can be successful in business and become wealthy, all in 9 simple steps. He has just completed the second book in the series, *Winning the Wealth Game Using Property*, a guide that shows you how you can make money with property. You won't believe how easy it is with this book!

About Glenn Wilson

Glenn Wilson is the Owner/Manager of a small business operating in the building industry. As an apprentice carpenter he achieved high grades and was awarded "Apprentice of the Year". His training gave him a thorough understanding of the broader building industry by working for three years in residential building and then another two years in the high-rise commercial building industry. He established his own business 15 years ago by opening his own workshop in carpentry and joinery. Through further study, this business developed to become "kitchen design, construction and installation" and was a finalist in a number of kitchen design and construction building awards. His further study gained him the full residential building licence. He now manages a highly successful kitchen design and construction business with a six figure annual turnover and his skills and expertise are highly sought after. He is energetic, self-motivated and forward thinking, always looking for new ideas and innovations both within his business and beyond.

Being self-employed, superannuation was an issue that Glenn had to deal with himself. He had saved a small portfolio and had invested this by putting his trust into a well-known, reputable managed fund trading shares on the Australian

Stock Market in a buy and hold manner. After five years of this method of investment Glenn was shocked to find that together with fees and charges he had only made 1% per year on his capital investment. At this stage Glenn was determined to find a better approach to investment that would achieve a far more acceptable yield.

In researching ways of building wealth using passive income he discovered Cooltrade on the web. This seemed to be an answer too good to be true but Glenn, being a cautious person wanted to prove to himself that the program did actually produce the results it was designed and claimed to produce.

Over the next few months he tested the program in detail and worked with the Cooltrade US team extensively to discover new methods of making the program better for Australian users. After running the program live for six months and becoming the first person in Australia to do so he was convinced that the program lived up to its expectations and had enormous potential for Australian investors.

This led him into discussions with Mark regarding marketing of the program throughout Australia and he offered his services as technical advisor. Because of the internet problems in Australia, Mark introduced Glenn to Daryl whose business was already a cloud provider. Following this, the company Cooltrade Australia with Mark, Glenn and Daryl was established.

Glenn's aim is to encourage many more average Australians to create wealth by becoming investors on the stock market and producing ongoing, passive income to supplement their wage or salary.

About Easen Evans

Easen Evans has had a job since he was 10 years old. Whether he was delivering newspapers or pizzas, selling sporting goods or construction specialists' time, Easen has always made life better for his customers. Picking up new skills in every one of his jobs, Easen has consistently looked for better ways to live a better life.

He and his wife found their better way to a better life by creating passive income streams for themselves so they can share their valuable time with their precious daughters. One of their most successful passive income streams is automated share trading.

By utilizing automated share trading software, they have the opportunity to actively enjoy their lifestyle without creating another "JOB" for themselves. Easen continues to help others discover their better way to a better life by providing them with the opportunity to achieve more than they ever thought possible; thereby......Winning the Wealth Game!

Other Books in the Series

Winning The Wealth Game In Business

Winning The Wealth Game With Property

Winning The Wealth Game by Protecting Your Assets

Winning the Wealth Game by Creating Multiple Streams of Income

Winning the Wealth Game Online

Winning the Wealth Game in Network Marketing

A Note From the Authors

Share trading has changed dramatically over the years. So much so that the average punter doesn't stand a chance. With computers performing 82% of all the share trades today it is a wonder we make any money at all.

Our goal in this book is to give you information on the types of strategies available and some background on share trading.

Our goal is also to open your mind to the possibility of having "robots" trade for you. By understanding that this is a possibility, it will allow you to get onto an even playing field with the big institutions. Making money is easy when you know the rules and even easier when you make then. Enjoy the book and be sure to take advantage of our special bonus offer as well.

To your trading success!

Mark, Glenn and Easen

Winning the Wealth Game With Shares

After the Great Financial Crisis of 2008-09, investors everywhere rightly feel nervous about markets. After all, wasn't it the irrational exuberance of investment bankers, inflating their paycheques with worthless securities that sent stock markets and credit markets into a tailspin?

Here's a little secret: the great investors of the world have been quietly buying into markets for months now. They see what's coming and are buying stocks that will double and triple in value over the next few years.

The simple truth is that opportunities abound today. There are companies – indeed countries – that are prospering right now and there are investors in the know who are profiting from the opportunity.

The transformation in share markets over recent decades has been truly amazing. Close to half of all adult people in the UK, in the USA and in Australia, own shares. Why do they do it? It's partly because the share market provides one of the best opportunities to achieve your long-term financial goals.

It's easy, you do not need a lot of money to get started, and shares give you flexibility and control.

When it comes down to connections wisdom, the key to wealth is quite simple. And no, it's not Lotto. Knowledge is the solution. Shares are an important part of any investment strategy and you will find that this book will help you to learn about the stock market and become a successful share investor.

Any investor can buy into a listed company: so you too can enjoy the powerful benefits that stock markets can bring. All you need is a good sense of money management and a sound knowledge of the basics of stock market investing.

First timers

You may never have been an investor; you may think that shares are for wealthy, knowledgeable people. You may believe that shares are the riskiest of all investments. On both counts you would be wrong. Indeed, shares are the safest investment of all asset classes - provided you approach this investment method in a methodical, step-by-step way; learning each step of the way; improving your knowledge, building your skills, learning to manage money and gaining all the time, the skills of an accomplished investor.

If you are now ready to make shares an effective part of your investment portfolio you need to answer a few key questions:

- What are my goals?
- How much money should I invest?
- How should I invest?
- What are the tax implications?

Each of these questions is highly particular to each individual but, in general, your age and stage and your capacity to fund a share investment strategy are important. Shares are safe in that you can keep your exposure very, very low while learning – as little as a $100. That may not ever amount to much but it will be a psychological start and just the beginning. If you add money progressively, say each month, it may be 12 months or more before you are investing significant amounts. That's the safety factor.

Now that you have a basic idea of what is involved and how to move forward, let's move onto the next chapter that defines exactly what shares are and how you can start making money with them. Good luck!

What are Shares?

If you searched the internet for the answer to this question, you may be surprised or daunted by the myriad of explanations and definitions that are supplied by the multitude of financial information websites. All of the definitions are correct – and would remain correct if they were replaced by the following statement. A share, or stock, as it's known in some parts of the world – represents a part, or fraction of ownership in a company.

When compared to the entire value of a company, an individual share is worth very little. However, owning multiple shares gives you a larger holding and increases your ownership, or stake in the company, which in turn, increases the value of your investment.

It would be safe to say at this point, that there is always an element of risk associated with either trading or investing in shares and this will be covered in more detail later on. In short, you should always seek the advice of a qualified professional before trading for the first time and also bear in mind that since the value of shares can fall as well as rise – sometimes rapidly - you could lose part, or even all, of your investment. There are precautions that can be taken to minimize losses and some of these are also covered later on, but still – always ensure that you are comfortable with what you are doing before taking your first trading steps. At the very least, the latest information is always available online and can be accessed at a time that suits you. If you don't have access to the internet, then you should try the financial section of your local library.

Background

In order to fully understand what shares are, it is also necessary to understand a little bit about how they are created – and therefore become available for buying and selling on a Stock Exchange.

When a company is initially formed, part of the company formation process involves the creation and allocation of shares. The allocation is then divided among a number of people who are then designated as company shareholders. These people, through their shareholdings, own the company and they may include the company directors, company secretaries, family members, friends, relatives or other investors.

It is important to note that whilst the shareholders own the company, they may not necessarily have control over the management, decision making and the day to day running of the business. This responsibility is allocated to a director or board of directors and they oversee the company's operation.

At some point during the life of a company, there may come a time when there is the need for a large injection of monetary income, or capital. This could be required for a variety of reasons such as the funding of future operations or expansion, for example. Capital may be obtained in any number of ways, outside of the general course of business. One very common way is to convert the company from a privately owned enterprise into a publicly owned one. Income obtained by the use of this method is known as equity financing.

The processes behind this conversion are extremely involved and complex – and in order to become a public company, a great deal of extensive criteria must be met. As such, these processes will not be discussed here in detail, since they are outside the scope of this article. However, there are a few parts to the process that are worthy of note.

At some point before the stock market launch, numerous decisions will have been made between the management team, the underwriters and any other involved parties, including how much of the company will be made available for sale to the public. When this happens, a portion of the company's shares are divided into smaller shares and it is these shares that will eventually be traded on the stock exchange.

Once the stock market launch takes place, the shares are put up for sale in the primary market. The primary market is a part of the stock exchange that mainly deals in the issuing of newly traded shares. This is known as underwriting.

Usually, there is a flurry of trading activity within the first few days – as traders and individuals buy up the shares. As they are bought up, the share price increases. This, in turn, increases the value of the company and raises the required capital, which is then available for the company to fund its operations or expansion, subsequently reducing the need to borrow from a bank or other financial institution.

You may already be familiar with many of the terms that are used at this time, such as flotation, stock market launch and Initial Public Offer, or IPO. These are commonly used in financial media reports when a high profile company decides to issue shares to the public for the first time.

Notable IPO's include The Agricultural Bank of China, raising over $19bn. By the time the first day's trading was over, the company was worth more than $100bn. Others include household names such as social networking giants Facebook and Twitter, Visa International and Google, to name but a few.

In addition to these, there have been equally high profile Government Privatizations of State-Owned companies, whether they be banks, airlines or other businesses. The Commonwealth Bank of Australia, British Airways, Air Canada and Rolls Royce – were all once government run.

Once issued, the shares are usually traded on the secondary market, or after–market and it is within this market that the majority of everyday trading takes place.

At the time of this writing, there are currently 21 major stock exchanges located in financial capitals around the world. There are also 81 other stock exchanges and yearly, the money that passes through them totals many trillions of dollars.

In the early days, shares certificates were issued on paper and had to be physically transferred from person to person to enact a trade. Nowadays, all share allocations, trades and transfers are processed electronically, thus speeding up the system greatly.

Once a trade order has been officially initiated, that is fully passed from broker to the electronic market, the purchase and selling of stocks happens within milliseconds. Electronic markets are continuously striving to lower the latency of trade completion times to astonishingly miniscule amounts of time.

There are numerous ways to buy shares and most commonly, one uses the services of a stockbroker. A stockbroker is essentially a middleman who arranges the transfer of shares from a buyer to a seller and vice versa. The stockbroker will charge a fee, or commission, for each trade.

Stockbrokers can provide either a full service or a discount service. Full service stockbrokers will be able to give you investment advice and offer you a more personal service – however, they will also usually charge a higher commission per trade in order to cover costs. A discount service stockbroker may offer little or no advice whatsoever. As a result, their commission charges are cheaper. When considering the speed of the sale or purchase of shares, a stockbroker often adds a considerable latency in comparison to direct to market sales, however the direct-to-market approach is often utilized only by professional day traders, as most people are not affected by this slight delay, and are benefited more by the convenience and advice of a stockbroker.

You may find that some of these services are named differently in certain countries, such as – discretionary, advisory and execution only service.

An advisory service operates in a similar fashion to a full service broker and an execution only service is similar to a discount broker. A discretionary service is a managed service whereby you employ the services of a professional to manage your portfolio for you. As a result, you will find that this service is usually more expensive.

Incidentally, there are many more factors regarding how much commission you will pay for each trade that you make. Again, these are outside the scope of this article and can be confusing for a new investor. Therefore, it is recommended that you should seek professional advice before proceeding.

As has been mentioned earlier in the text, the value of shares can go up, or down. Once again, there are many factors that can cause the price of a share to move and two of the most common ones are supply and demand and market sentiment.

Supply and demand is quite easy to understand and a brief explanation is provided below – albeit a simplistic one.

If the shares for a particular company are in short supply – maybe due to the fact that the price has recently risen dramatically for whatever reason - then the demand for them will also increase. It can be considered that they are worth investing in because the price is rising.

When this happens, investors will hold onto the shares that they buy, hoping that the price – and thus the value - will continue to rise further.

Since investors are holding onto their shares, demand outweighs supply and the shares become scarcer. As such, both the price and value will continue to increase.

Eventually, a limit will be reached – either because there are no more shares for sale or certain investors believe that the price will start to fall soon and they feel the time has come to sell, making the most profit possible. As the price starts to fall, the flow of shares into the market increases and demand wanes accordingly.

Another factor that can alter the price of a share is something called Market Sentiment.

Market sentiment is not as easy to understand as supply and demand. You may be familiar with terms including the words "bull" and "bear".

In general, a positive attitude from investors towards the market is known as "bullish" sentiment. In direct opposition to this, a general negative attitude towards it is known as "bearish" sentiment.

It may seem bizarre that something as simple as a general mood can have so much effect on the world economy, but this can and does happen. If a highly respected market analyst predicts that a certain company will report a record profit, then it is fair to assume that the share price will rise on the strength of the analyst's prediction.

Advantages and Disadvantages

In short, if the markets can be so volatile, then a beginner could be forgiven for asking the question, "Why would I want to risk investing money in shares, when I can place it in a bank account, where it's safer?"

This is a question with numerous answers and there are many advantages and disadvantages to buying, selling and investing in shares.

Starting with the two main disadvantages.

- Since ordinary shareholders are the last people to be compensated in the event of a company going bankrupt, you could lose all of your money if that were to happen.

This is known as absolute risk – and the prospect of losing all of your money is an extremely daunting one. Whilst it is true that one may buy and hold shares in one company, and one company alone, it is both usual and normal to buy shares in multiple companies in different market sectors. Market sectors are explained in more detail later on, but basically, they are groups of companies that are similar enough to be classed as direct competitors. For example, a single sector could consist of industries that deal with farming and agriculture – although sector classification varies from country to country. Buying shares in many different sectors is known as Diversification. By using diversification as a method for the management of your portfolio, you spread the risk and thus minimize the possibility of losing all of your money in the event of a single company failure (we'll talk about the proper way to diversify investments later in this book).

- You could lose some, or most of your money if the market experiences a sudden downturn.

Believe it or not, this disadvantage is a little easier to cope with. The value of your shares will rise and fall over the time that you hold onto them. Sometimes the rises and falls will be slight but at other times, they may be severe. Whilst the value of your shares may be 50% more or 50% less than what they were when you initially purchased them, the only time you will lose money on them, is when you actually sell them. It is always possible that the price will rally, or rise. However, if you feel that the share price will continue to drop, then you must be prepared to cut your losses – even if you find that you were eventually wrong and the price rises once more. Never hold on to a stock whilst hoping for the best.

On a lighter note, there are also many advantages that should be considered.

- In return for investing their money into a company, shareholders can receive certain benefits.

If a company returns a profit at the end of their financial year, the management can decide whether to pay a dividend on its shares. This means that part of the profits are divided up and paid to shareholders – essentially as a share of the profits. This can be made as a cash payment or the amount can be paid by the issuing of new or bonus shares. Certain companies, mainly those from the retail sector, allow shareholders to receive a discount on goods and services that are purchased from their own stores.

- Capital Appreciation.

Capital growth occurs when the value of a share rises above the initial purchase price. Any profit made when a share is sold is called Capital Gains. As such, you may be liable for Capital Gains Tax and you should seek the advice of an accountant to determine how much tax you may have to pay.

- The rate of growth of a share is usually greater than the return from a bank account.

Since share prices have the potential to rise quite rapidly, in certain cases, the return is greater than that given by a bank.

- No liability for the debts of the company.

As a shareholder, you have no liability for the debts of a company in which you have invested. Your risk is covered by the equity in the shares alone and if the company goes into liquidation, the maximum amount that you can lose is the value of the shares.

In any eventuality, you are ultimately responsible for the management of your portfolio and must be aware of the value of your shares and must also be aware of market trends. As an investor, it would be considerably irresponsible to buy shares in random companies that had not been researched to some degree and to leave them in the hope that the share prices will rise exponentially, thus maximizing the return on your investment. As with most things, the more time you are willing to invest, the more market experience you will gain.

Why Own Shares?

If you ask most people why they invest in shares, chances are their answer will revolve around the money that can be made in the share market. However, I believe that the reason to invest in shares is more subtle than that - shares are a great inflation hedge.

Inflation is the depreciation of the purchasing power on the dollar. We see this concept manifest itself as prices increase at the gas pumps, grocery stores, car dealerships, and so on. You may remember that stamps used to be thirteen cents in the 1970s, new cars were a couple of thousand dollars, and a new house cost around $25,000 dollars. The cost of goods and services are continually rising due largely to inflation.

What most of us don't realize, or think about, is that we actually own the entities that are raising prices when we *own* shares. To understand the significance of this, we must look at the *P/E ratio*. You may have heard of the P/E ratio before— it is simply a reflection of the amount of money the market is willing to pay for each dollar of earnings from a company. "P" stands for "price" and "E" represents "earnings," so it is the ratio of the market value (or price) per share to the earnings per share.

Stock market analysts often use this statistic to make sure the price they are paying for a stock is reasonable. Calculating a stock's P/E ratio is easy. If a stock is selling for $50 dollars per share (P), and has earnings of $5 dollars per share (E), then its P/E ratio is:

P/E Ratio = 50 / 5 = **10 (or 10/1)**

This tells us that traders are willing to pay $10 dollars for every $1 dollar in earnings.

Taking a deeper look, we can see why shares can help protect us against inflation. As mentioned earlier, in the P/E ratio, the "E" in the denominator is "earnings." From accounting class, we learned how to arrive at earnings:

> **Earnings** = Sales – Cost of Goods Sold – General Operating Expenses – Interest – Expenses – Taxes – Etc… And with this calculation, we'll get down to the company's earnings.

When the dollar depreciates, companies raise their prices to make sure they are getting fairly paid for their products and services. That means the "sales" number in the formula above will go up. Of course, all the other numbers will most likely go up as well. Eventually, the company will make sure the earnings increase—they must in order to stay in business. This will positively affect the price of the stock; therefore, it will provide inflation protection.

For example, if a company has a P/E ratio of 15/1, and the dollar's purchasing power is cut in half, the company in question will start to raise prices. This will drive up the "sales" figure and eventually their earnings will double. All else being equal, the share price will have to rise to $30 dollars to keep the P/E ratio the same (15/1 = 30/2). As you can see in our example, our stock price doubled when costs doubled. This is not to say that stocks necessarily benefit over the short run from inflationary environments, but in the long run, they protect investors against inflation far better than other investments.

Stock Prices and the Market

The stock market is largely driven by supply and demand. Thus, stock prices are literally set by a willing buyer and a willing seller agreeing on the fair price for the stock they are trading. There is a formula that can help you get an idea of what kind of information traders use to determine if the price is right for a stock. It is called the *Gordon Growth Formula*, named after Professor Myron J. Gordon of the University of Toronto. It is calculated in the following way:

The Gordon Growth Formula:

$$P = D \times (1 + G) / (R - G)$$

Price = Dividend $\times$ (1 + Growth Rate) / (Cost of Capital − Growth Rate)

Although the model has some obvious flaws, it is quite useful for understanding many of the price movements we see in the stock market. (By the way, there won't be a test on the formula.)

Let's say we have a company with an expected dividend of $1 dollar, a cost of capital of 10 percent, and a growth rate of 5 percent. The Gordon Growth Model would determine the price as follows:

$$P = 1 \times (1 + .05) / (.10 - .05)$$

$$P = \$21$$

Thus, the model suggests that we would pay $21 dollars for the stock.

To understand how fresh economic information can move the market, let's take a look at a few real-life headlines and articles, and then we'll see how this news can cause changes in stock prices. Keep in mind that I'm using over-simplified numbers to make the math easy, and I changed the company names to protect the innocent. (Please note: The bold/underlined words used below are my own emphasis, not from the articles):

> "**XYZ Company** issued a **weak outlook** amid softness in the Australian housing market and a broader economic slowdown. Its shares **tumbled**."

If the previous estimate of growth was 5 percent, we might now conclude that the new number should be somewhat lower. Perhaps growth may be expected to go down to 4 percent in the future. Here's what happens when we plug in the new number:

Price = Dividend x (1 + Growth Rate) / (Cost of Capital – Growth Rate)

Dividend = $1

Cost of Capital = 10% (based on risk and inflation)

Growth Rate = 4%

Price = 1 x (1 + .05) / (.10 – **.04**)

Price = $17.50

Our stock has dropped in value from $21 dollars to $17.50 based on some bad news about future growth prospects.

Now let's look at a different set of circumstances, again using a real headlines (but fake numbers):

Optimism on Australian Economy Spurs a Global Rebound

"Stocks rose around much of the world in the third quarter, recouping steep losses from previous months **as <u>fears</u> about inflation and higher Australian interest rates <u>moderated</u>.**"

The first thing to notice here is that investors' fears have *moderated* or lessened. This often means that they reduce their cost of capital requirements. In other words, investors can't really demand high rates of return when the risk isn't there. The current owners of the stock would rather continue to hang on than accept a price that is too low for their shares.

Remember, before that our cost of capital number was 10 percent. Now we'll assume that it goes down to 9 percent.

Price = Dividend x (1 + Growth Rate) / (Cost of Capital – Growth Rate)

Dividend = $1

Cost of Capital = 9% (based on risk & inflation)

Growth Rate = 5%

Price = 1 x (1 + .05) / (**.09** − .05)

Price = $26.25

In this case, our stock jumped in value (from $21 dollars to $26.50) based on a difference in the perceived risk of investing. We will pay more for stocks when we feel safer, and since we'll pay more, the long-term growth potential is reduced.

How to make sense of share prices?

Have you ever been to an auction? Have you ever bargained with a market treader? Why do oil prices fluctuate? It seems perplexing and mysterious; but essentially you need to understand that many factors can simultaneously affect values both positively and negatively over different periods of time. However, the impact of many individual factors is sometimes quite predictable so it can pay to consider them since that is what many other investors will be doing.

Think of the price of a share as being affected by:

- Supply of and demand for the shares
- The inherent value of the shares (a subject for further study)
- Other less direct influences on share prices.

The share market is a market place like any other. The forces of supply and demand determine the price of shares. The more people want to get hold of a particular share, the higher its price will go. If people no longer want a share and few people are willing to buy it, people may have to offer it at a very low price in order to sell it.

Why Do Stocks Fluctuate?

As you can see, stocks are constantly moving up and down in value based on new information being processed by traders. Investors are always trying to get a handle on what profits are going to be in the future and the related risks involved. If there is good news, stocks will adjust upward to reflect that news. When the news is bad—prices will go down. Since professional traders do the vast majority of buying and selling in exchanges around the world, this information is often reflected in stock prices extremely quickly.

One of the key points that I stress is this: Any time you see a need to sell stocks, remember that there is someone out there that wants to buy the stocks you are unloading. The same works in reverse—when you get excited about buying, there is always someone waiting to sell them to you.

The Cost of Capital

At its core, the capital markets (also known as the stock and bond markets) are giant machines for raising money for companies who need it. Put simply, companies want access to your capital and they are willing to pay for the use of your money. The rate of return you can expect will vary based on the risks involved and the inflation rate—and the higher the risk or inflation rate, the higher the expected return.

When it comes to bonds, the cost of capital is easy to determine. All you have to do is look at the interest rate that the company, government, or other borrower is paying to figure out their cost of capital. If they are paying six percent on their bonds, then their cost of capital is six percent, or $6 dollars per year for every $100 dollars borrowed. In most cases (unless the bond is a variable rate bond), the interest payment will remain the same over the life of the loan. In this case, the lender will receive $60 dollars every year.

With stocks, calculating the cost of capital is not quite that simple. Instead of receiving regular interest payments, the owner of the stock is a participant in the earnings of the company. The board of directors doesn't send you a check for all the earnings every year, but they do often pay dividends. What isn't paid as a dividend goes back into the company—of which we own a part.

With that in mind, we can look at the P/E ratio in a whole new light. Historically, the average P/E ratio is around 15/1. That means that I'm buying $1 dollar of earnings for each $15 dollars that I pay. If I turn that fraction upside down (like I did with the bond), I've got a 1 to 15 ratio or 1 ÷ 15 = 6.67 percent. (Remember the bond paid $6 dollars for each $100 dollars invested, and I could calculate my interest rate by dividing 6 by 100.)

A Critical Difference between Stocks and Bonds

It has often been said that stocks are just bonds in disguise. The difference with the bond interest payment and the earnings that I get with the stock is that I have a fighting chance that the stock's earnings will rise over time. The bond issuer has no obligation to pay me any more interest than they agreed to when they borrowed the money. Therefore higher returns are possible with stocks due to their potential earnings growth, which is not the case with bonds.

How high has that return been? Historically, large U.S. stocks have provided a rate of return in the ten percent range. To put it a different way, their cost of capital has been around ten percent. If we look at any thirty-year period from the mid 1920's to today, we see that the ten percent varies minimally over this span, and many other asset categories have actually provided higher returns. This is interesting because the period in question contains some pretty ominous events, among them: The Great Depression, World War II, The Korean War, The Cuban Missile Crisis, The Vietnam War, The Oil Crisis, The Gulf War, and The Iraq War.

Risks of Investing in Stock

It is often said that there is no return without risk—and we all know this. I doubt anyone would ever invest in a CD again if they knew they could get stock market returns with CD-level risk, but that is not reality. Although stocks tend to protect us against inflation risks, they—of course—present us with other risks.

One risk of investing in stocks is called non-systematic risk. This is also known as a diversifiable risk. It is the risk of losing money in an individual stock. History is full of examples of companies that have gone bankrupt or had severe drops in value due to circumstances that were unique to those companies. For example, when Kmart went bankrupt, it didn't have a negative impact on other retailers. When GM and Ford face difficulties, that doesn't mean that Toyota is going to have problems. When E.F. Hutton talks, people don't listen. Stocks can drop in value because of competitive pressures, mismanagement, lawsuits, financial troubles, or any number of issues that affect only the company involved.

One recent study conducted by a group of esteemed professors found that firm-level volatility (the volatility of individual stocks) from 1962 to 1997 more than doubled, but the volatility of the overall market during that time changed very little. In other words, stocks are more volatile than they used to be—in both directions—but the market doesn't move up and down any more than it used to.

This suggests that stocks seem to be offsetting each other. When one company drops dramatically, it is just as likely that another company's stock will shoot up in value. The bottom line is that it takes more stocks to be truly diversified in the present-day economy. In fact, one part of the study showed that portfolios with more stocks could have less risk and still end up with greater returns.

The other type of risk involved with stock investing is systematic risk. This is simply the upward and downward movement that we see in the market. It's like the up and down movement of the ocean. When the tide comes in, all boats rise. When it ebbs, they fall. The biggest difference is that the movement of the market is not even as remotely predictable as ocean currents. To further explain this, think of stocks moving like a school of fish (as if you need another analogy).

Sometimes you wonder who's following whom as they go up and down in value.

Market risk can't really be avoided, unless of course you decide not to invest in the market at all. The risk can be reduced somewhat, however, by diversifying across different areas of the stock market.

Cost of Capital and Risk

A company's cost of capital is easy to determine with bonds. Simply look at the interest rates on borrowed money to determine what their cost of capital is. If a company has one foot on a banana peel and the other in bankruptcy court, they are going to pay more when they borrow money than a more stable company.

We can often get a glimpse of a company's cost of capital on the stock side when we look at other financial ratios. For instance, a company's price-to-book value can be a useful tool for this purpose.

The concept of book value is simple:

Book Value = Assets − Liabilities

Book value is just the value of what a company *owns* minus what they *owe*. Most companies are worth more than the value of their land, buildings, machinery, and other assets minus their debts, so they usually sell for more than their book value. Like the P/E ratio, the price-to-book value is also expressed as a fraction: P/B. If a company is selling at or near their book value, this is a sign that investors don't have much confidence in the company.

The price-to-earnings (P/E) ratio can also be used to help investors understand cost of capital. It has some practical limitations, but it helps make this concept clearer. Since the P/E ratio tells us how much investors are paying for each dollar of earnings, it follows that it also tells us how much the person selling the stock must give away to get your money. (Note: It is only when the company is doing an initial public offering—that is, when the company is raising money by selling stock to the public—that your money actually goes to the company. Most of the time, when we buy stock, our money goes to another investor who is selling their holdings.)

Often, investors get excited about investing in some company that has a product line or service that they like. Perhaps they see big lines every time they go to the one of its locations or hear great things about the company's future. What they often fail to realize is that everyone else notices it as well and are paying a premium for each dollar of earnings.

One popular company I use as an example has a current P/E ratio of 50 to 1—let's call it BuyMoreCo. Investors are paying $50 dollars for every $1 dollar of BuyMoreCo earnings. Another less popular company, called LowSalesCo, is selling for $10 dollars to every $1 dollar of earnings.

Here's an interesting way to look at this: The owners/stockholders of LowSalesCo get five times less money for the same level of earnings. To get $50 dollars, an owner of LowSalesCo would have to give up the rights to receive $5 dollars of earnings verses the owner of the BuyMoreCo giving up only $1 dollar.

All else being equal, LowSalesCo has a much higher cost of capital than BuyMoreCo because their owners have to give away more in profits for each dollar raised (assuming profits don't change over the next year). This should remind us of bond investing. The entity that pays more in interest (pays more dollars for each dollar borrowed) has a higher cost of capital than the entity that pays less interest. The difference in cost of capital can also be seen when we examine the two companies' earnings yields. BuyMoreCo's earnings yield is 1/50 or two percent. LowSalesCo's earnings yield is 1/10 or ten percent.

Here is how it looks:

BuyMoreCo P/E   50/1   LowSalesCo P/E
10/1   10/1 x 5/5 = 50/5

The little known technique for staying ahead of the game

Sometimes investors simply are blind to what makes a successful investor. It comes down to one fundamental principle and it's a very easy technique to apply once you are into your strides: *only buy into good businesses.*

The direct impact on a company's share price is the performance of its businesses. Many large businesses like Shell and BHP-Billiton are doing well and continue to please investors (that is not disappoint them with bad news); thus a share price will generally increase in value. It may move around somewhat in the day to day buying and selling and especially move around if boarder economic indicators like a credit crunch impact a market as a whole. Successful companies are businesses that re-invest in their future. They are growing their businesses continuously.

In other words, a share that offers a strong likelihood of capital growth due to reinvesting company profits also has a certain amount of inherent value. The most important factor affecting the price of a share is the company's future earnings prospects, as its earnings will determine the future inherent value of a share. Any changes in forecast earnings, either by company management or by market analysts, will impact the share price.

Past earnings, as can be found in the company's annual report, are an important indicator of a company's earnings ability, but you should also consider the impact of any changes to its business. For example, how will it be affected by a change in senior management, or an acquisition of another business?

Large markets like the New York market which is often reported in terms of a basket of stocks known as the Dow Jones Industrial Average (DJIA) are closely monitored around the world and can impact other markets. This is due to the sheer size of the US stock market as it dwarfs other markets many times over due to the fact that the US is a huge economy but also because many investors (large institutional as well as private) hold shares in American companies.

In a similar fashion (although not anywhere near as globally impactful), the UK stock market is often reported on by a broad index of stock known as the FTSE and it can impact European markets because London has long been a centre of banking and trade finance for the Continent. It remains one of the world's oldest and largest stock exchanges.

Australia for example (and increasingly India and China), is becoming a progressively significant investment market. Australians resource companies are among the largest in the world and many global investors are seeing that India and China have massive populations seeking to expand their economies and see Australian companies as a proxy for these other countries.

The Advantages of Large Businesses

Larger banks and companies who perform a great amount of trades per day often utilize robotic trading software. These companies can afford to pay teams of engineers to specifically design algorithms and tweak servers and high level computers to compute the best trades and perform them within milliseconds.

These software programs, often called High-Frequency Trading Software, are often questioned on their ethical status and their possible ability to artificially hike prices and sell instantaneously.

One example of the possible effects of High-Frequency Trading Software is the "Flash Crash" of 2010. On May 6th, around the time of the Greek Debt Crisis, the DOW market experienced a dramatic decline of around 300 points. Over the span of roughly five minutes, from 2:42 to 2:57, the market dropped an incredible 600 points more! It was only ten minutes later that the market had recovered those 600 points, creating what was surely a very stressful period of time for anyone closely watching their stocks at the time.

Although High-Frequency software can't be solely blamed for the event, the software did contribute to the sudden drop when the various algorithms panicked and sold their holdings, only to possibly repurchase them a short time afterwards as the market rebounded.

The Impact of Electronic Trading

The Information Age brought about a great change in nearly all aspects of life, from instant mailing of documents to long distance phone calls that can be made nearly anywhere. It's no big surprise that financial services are also changing to a quicker digital alternative.

Personal computing devices have brought about a major change to how stock trading can be accomplished. These days, anyone with a few dollars and an internet connection can purchase shares of companies they may have never even heard of operating from any corner of the globe.

It's important to remember that the internet contains a wealth of information and possibilities, but not everything is equally appropriate for any situation.

As you become more accustomed to the stock markets, it may be of great value for you to spend a little time every now and then researching financial news and reading market headlines. Not everything out there may be interesting or of value to you, and a portion of it may not even make sense right now. Just like any other skill or acquired bit of knowledge, continued study can dramatically improve your ability to know why things are occurring and give you a sense of what to expect when major news events and crises occur.

This book can be a great tool in your kit to begin understanding the markets, terminology, and ideas behind your trading, but it should be complimented with a quick study of current events every so often. If nothing else, a good base knowledge of events will help prevent you from being swept up in a panic should you come across an alarming sensationalist story your odd cousin posted on your favourite social media website.

The Psychology of Trading

Interestingly, a lot of the time we see people buying high and selling low. Even at first glance, without needing further analysis, it is clear that this cannot be a profitable strategy. Trading psychology has a considerable influence on the behavior of traders and requires a complete understanding in order to avoid falling into a spiral of accumulating losses.

For many entering the market for the first time, trading may appear to simply be a mathematical game. In other words, if you use the right numbers and make accurate calculations, you will end up coming out on top. But this explanation does not address why traders will continue to lose in the market. If it is simply a matter of mathematics and everyone has access to the same data, then everyone should end up with the right answer and the most profitable trading results.

The issue is *how* the numbers are interpreted. The data might not be misleading, but the mind can and will play tricks at times. Your individual hopes and fears will skew your thinking and actions.

The psychology of trading may be said to have a larger impact on trading activity than the actual methodology used. Continuously poor trading results are often attributable to a psychological problem and not the trading method. A successful trader has to be mentally prepared to accept the risks inherent in financial trading. An important step in this psychological preparation is to recognize the importance of trading psychology and accept that psychological issues, if not adequately addressed, can hinder the trading method. Trading involves various emotions (e.g. fear, confusion and despair) that can become quite overwhelming.

The worlds of trading and psychology do overlap and are quite complex. Performance anxiety is a psychological factor that can seriously hinder a trader trying to make an important market decision. It does not matter how clear headed a trader is seen to be – or how clear headed you see yourself to be – anxiety can negatively influence trading performance.

Buying high and selling low occurs as a result of emotional trading; this type of trading has no place in the markets if you expect to make a decent living from your financial transactions. The accumulation of losses often starts as a result of fear.

Traders are afraid of failing in the market and their actions begin to be led by their emotions. As a consequence, the confidence of a trader can plummet to great depths.

As a trader, you have to be able to know yourself completely and identify your strengths and weaknesses. By doing this, you can rely on your strengths to make profitable trades in the market and learn to control your weaker points. By using this psychological approach, you can be on your way to becoming a successful trader.

The market environment is constantly changing, especially the currency market. Having adequate and accurate knowledge of yourself and an understanding of how you will react when particular market conditions are present, will allow you to put measures in place to protect yourself from decisions that can harm your portfolio.

Overall, poor trading practices in the market can increase levels of stress. An example of such a practice is taking too much risk with large lot sizes. By repeatedly not giving much thought to the money being put at risk and not analyzing the market conditions appropriately, a trader can become very frustrated.

Even traders who are grounded and base their moves in the market on solidly thought out methods may be influenced by psychological factors. They may find that the tactics they have chosen are not compatible with their current talents and skills.

In addition, a particular type of trade may not be suitable for a particular type of trader. For instance, a trader who has highly analytical and risk adverse traits may experience great stress by using aggressive, short-term methods of market scalping.

The method may seem to be theoretically relevant, but may in fact be completely inappropriate for some types of traders. It is easy for aggressive trading to become disastrous for an individual who likes to place safe bets.

An interesting fact is that issues of trading psychologically may not actually have much to do with trading. Therefore, varying trading methods will not always solve psychological problems. Instead, a trader will have to understand, acknowledge and learn to control their anxiety and emotions, as well as build discipline.

If there is only one thing you learn about trading psychology that will help you in the market, it is that:

- *YOU* are your biggest enemy while trading.

Forget about the market, the big players in the market or significant economic happenings and world affairs. There will be no recovery from being a consistent loser if you continuously make the wrong decisions and experience multiple losses because you have not developed a professional trading psychology.

- *Discipline* involves having a well laid out plan to ensure that expected downsides and upturns are accounted for.

A good trader will not be unduly influenced by his/her own excitement or fear or another person's advice on what or how to trade. Experience will teach a trader that there are times when it is more advantageous to be watching the market from the sidelines, simply biding your time until it is profitable to enter the market once again. Do not lose sight of your own system that you have in place and the technical knowledge that you have developed.

- ***Emotional detachment* is an essential characteristic for a successful trader.**

Instead of manically checking prices throughout the day and giving too much thought to every little move in the market or every snippet of market news, an emotionally detached trader will wait for signals and watch large trends before calmly using the system they have in place to make the appropriate decision. Your mind should not be engaged with even one extra factor that has little, or no, importance. It is more useful to stay focused on the bigger picture so that you are not bogged down with the niggling details that may throw your emotions off track.

Good trading psychology involves the realization that you will not be able to predict everything that will happen in the market. You can only learn to understand the events that may occur, try to be prepared for them and equip yourself to take the relevant actions.

The psychology of trading should not be viewed as an excuse for losing. In actuality, it is a phenomenon which requires understanding in order to prevent large losses and the 'buy high, sell low" scenario. Financial trading is inherently risky in nature, and traders have a better chance of minimizing losses and maximizing profits once they are psychologically prepared to trade.

Remember that losses will always be a part of the trading process. However, minimizing these losses is the key to successful trading activity. Profitable trading requires an understanding of the psychological issues involved so that "buy high, sell low" strategies can be avoided.

How you are at an advantage...

Momentum is an important consideration in trading. As a trader, you need to always follow momentum. This concept is the reason why you have an advantage over the "big boys" in the business.

As an individual trader, there is one tremendous advantage that you have over institutional investors and even large scale portfolio managers as well. Once you recognize this advantage, you can revise your trading strategies on the stock market so that you can benefit from some situations in the way that institutional investors simply cannot.

The market to be in will vary according to what is happening at a particular time. It may be Asia, the United States, Europe, etc., and a good trader will always be able to identify the more attractive markets at any given time.

We need to follow momentum because we need to know which markets are rising the fastest and the reasons why they are rising the fastest. These movements occur because of the amount of money being moved into certain markets.

A trend develops which may start off as a straight line, then begin to slip and sometimes spiral as it did during the global financial crisis of 2008, and we would go to cash.

A movement of this type requires appropriate protection from the downside. A reverse position can be considered if the market shows signs of moving up again.

You may be wondering about all of this advice and questioning why it is that the "big boys" in the business do not already do what I am proposing. Why is it that JP Morgan does not do this? What about Merrill Lynch? Barclays? What about any other banks or financial institutions?

As an individual stock trader, you may not have been aware of any particular advantage that you have over the "big boys". However, you might be very conscious of the advantages possessed by institutional traders.

Institutional investors have a tremendous amount of information about companies available to them. They can also afford to pay for this information if necessary. These types of traders can be provided with a large volume of current and accurate information from assistance traders, economists and researchers. They obviously have an edge over other types of traders with regard to information.

An individual stock market trader does not have easy access to company information which is often private. In addition, this type of trader cannot rely on information which appears to be based on rumors and lacks properly confirmed sources.

An individual trader will not have the resources available to have the news confirmed and this cost may not be reasonable based on the size of the trading capital that is allocated for that particular stock.

Institutional traders can access a large number of markets. It is quite common for them to use vendors, such as Bloomberg and Reuters, to monitor many global markets. However, a retail trader would be discouraged by the high exchange data fees which may not make much financial sense.

A lot of banks either possess their own in-house execution platform or utilize a high-end platform, such as Trading Technologies, GL Trade or Pats. In addition, their execution speed is more than likely to be faster than that of the retail trader based on the internet.

The advantage these companies hold can often seem to be similar to the famous U.S. monopoly Standard Oil, who often utilized its large financial force to shove around smaller businesses and purchase illegal transportation contracts. Standard Oil eventually drove most of the competition out of business and dominated until 1911 when the U.S. Supreme Court declared it an illegal monopoly and began sanctions to shrink and disable its influence.

Our modern-day financial giants may seem to be menacing, like Standard Oil was during its time, but despite their deep pockets the individual trader still has many tools available to level the playing field, and the bureaucracy and sheer size of these companies can limit their ability to implement changes in strategy as quickly as the individual can.

Institutional traders also benefit from a pooling of knowledge. They work with other traders, which can facilitate useful discussions of market information. In this way, each trader can learn from the other.

Strategies that are heavily reliant on capital and high-end software can be carried out easily by institutional traders. They are commonly able to average down to build a position and implement arbitrage strategies, which can end up being low-risk, consistent and quite profitable.

Yet, in spite of all these advantages of institutional trading, an individual stock trader does have a vital edge over the institutional investor.

The reason the JP Morgan's, Merrill Lynch's, Barclays and other financial institutions in the market do not follow the advice given earlier in the chapter about following momentum is because of the difference in their trading capital. With regard to momentum, the smaller size of capital becomes an advantage for the individual stock traders and becomes a disadvantage for the institutional investor.

Institutional investors cannot take the same actions as individual stock traders because they ARE the market. With the amount of money that these institutions are managing, if they try putting it in cash the entire market would crash.

It is difficult for an institutional investor to enter into or exit from a stock without a significant change to the price of the shares because of the huge amount of capital that is allocated to it; every stock market transaction and trade has an impact on the stock's share price. The significance of the impact is dependent on the number of the shares being transacted in relation to the counter party. Therefore, an institutional investor will find it more and more difficult to manage short term trades because the trading capital keeps accumulating as investors increasingly add funds to it. This phenomenon may also explain why some institutional investors only give long-term trading advice on stocks; they are simply unable to do otherwise.

On the other hand, an individual stock trader or investor does not have to be bothered about a limitation of this type. Mistaken entries can be quickly corrected without making too big a loss as a result. An individual trader can also benefit from large price moves in the short-term that occur when they make a mistake. An institutional investor cannot take these actions without either reducing capital or giving tips to small-scale traders-

As an individual stock trader, you have a wonderful advantage over the "big boys" who seem to control the daily stock market prices. This is a weakness of theirs that you should seek to exploit to your advantage.

A good tip for an investor is to put their money with a strong, secured financial institution in which they have confidence. Then people like us can manage their funds because we have the ability to move in and out of the market at will without affecting it in the way that the major institutions would.

Our advantage over the "big boys" in the market is that we can follow momentum. We can move quietly within the market and use our abilities to profitably manage funds.

Eliminating the Psychology

Before you become overwhelmed by the thought of risking your hard earned savings, it may be beneficial at this point to tell you a story about a guy named Ed Barsano. Ed was a former Microsoft employee who retired with a very large amount of money, only to lose millions during the "Tech Bubble Burst" in the early 2000's.

Along with thousands of others who had lost money around this period of time, Ed was in need of a way to recover from this unfortunate event. Ed decided that he should set out and again put his software engineering skills back to good use, so he began developing a software program that could detect and prevent losses like this from happening. The program being developed was his own version of a fully automated trading system, similar to what some large multi-billion dollar banks are utilizing.

About four years (and millions of lines of code) later, he produced a software program called Cooltrade, which had the capacity to be given a trading strategy, and autonomously carry out purchases and the selling of shares in order to minimize loss. With a program like this, he wouldn't have to worry about sudden crashes. Cooltrade was able to detect and sell early if it detected trouble!

Ed decided that rather than hoard this trading advantage as a secret, as the other larger, wealthier companies have with done their own versions of High-Frequency Trading Software, he would do something revolutionary. Ed released his software to the public sector.

His software was initially picked up by many other software engineers, along with professional day traders, who all began to add their own strategies and tactics into the program. Due to the open nature of the Cooltrade program, these strategies were saved into a library and are available as part of an ever increasing collection of strategies that anyone who has the Cooltrade program can utilize. Cooltrade has become one of a very small number of automated trading software systems that are openly available to the public. What may be even more impressive is Cooltrade's long proven record of reliability.

Remember the "Flash Crash" of 2010, when the DOW market dropped about 900 points, the majority of which happened over 5 minutes? As the market dipped and recovered shortly afterwards by hundreds of points, Ed's Cooltrade software was able to take advantage of both sides of the crash. Cooltrade reacted quickly enough to sell shares as they fell, and knew to purchase as the market was recovering. The power of Automated Trading Software such as Cooltrade is becoming increasingly impressive as more and more people begin utilizing and sharing their strategies. Each of these strategies are tested and recorded, so that a newcomer only needs to select a desired strategy from a library.

Revisiting the software and systems that Institutional Traders are using to gain an advantage and accrue their large, steady profits, you can now be aware that you can have a similar advantage as an individual trader.

Although the individual trader does not have the massive funding to purchase enormous volumes of steadily accruing stocks, with the use of your own robotic trading software you can autonomously maintain purchase and sales of smaller quantities of stocks with a greatly reduced time investment and stress level.

The personal usage of a fully automated trading system such as Cooltrade can be explained through the use of a silly allegory. Imagine a contest of skill between a nimble swordsman and a hulking brute who wields a massive hammer. Although the brute can swing terrifying and crushing weight around, as he effectively demolishes his targets, the swordsman has a unique advantage in speed due to his smaller size and lighter weapon. With the proper strategy in mind, the swordsman can quickly identify the beginnings of the brute's attacks, and move to counter and dodge them with ease. As effective and terrifying as the brute may seem, the size of its weapon gives subtle hints as to where it will move next while the brute gathers force for its next swing.

The Cooltrade platform is much like the swordsman to the large Institutional Trader's brute. The software can quickly identify, sell, and purchase stocks according to a preset strategy. While the other large Institutional Traders are beginning to shift their larger sums towards a growing target fund, boosting gains before it just as quickly identifies a downward shift and sells for profit.

Visuals

You must have heard the phrase "a picture is worth a thousand words" before. Well, with trading there is no exception. Charts can help to identify significant trends so you can decide whether or not to risk your money on a particular trade.

The more common types of stock trading charts are:

* Bar chart OHLC (open, high, low and close price);

  Each bar shows the opening, highest, lowest and closing price, which could be on a daily, weekly, monthly or other basis. It is simple, quick and easy to interpret.

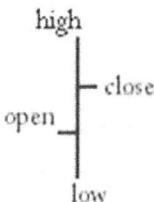

Open represents the first price traded and is shown by the horizontal foot located on the left side of the bar.

The highest price traded during the bar is indicated by "high" at the top of the vertical bar.

Low is represented at the bottom of the vertical bar and is the lowest price traded during the bar.

The horizontal foot located on the right side of the bar refers to the last price traded during the bar, or close.

The locations of the opening and closing feet will indicate the direction of the bar. It is a downward bar if the closing foot is below the opening foot and an upward bar if the closing foot is above the opening foot.

The chart above shows that the opening price is lower than the closing price.

The range of the bar is indicated by the distance between the top and bottom of the bar. It is calculated by subtracting the low from the high.

- Japanese candlestick

As with the bar chart, the candlestick bar shows the opening, highest, lowest and closing price, which could be based on any chosen time frame. They are also known for their ease of reading and interpretation.

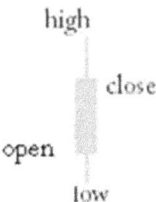

high

close

open

low

The first price traded during the candlestick is represented by the open which is located at either the top or the bottom of the wide vertical line. It will be found at the top for a downward candlestick or at the bottom for an upward candlestick, as in the one above.

The high is found at the top of the thin vertical bar (or wick of the candlestick) and is the highest price traded during the candlestick.

The lowest price traded during the candlestick is indicated by the low located at the bottom of the thin vertical bar (or upside down wick of the candlestick).

The close can be found at either the top or bottom of the wide vertical line and indicates the last price traded during the candlestick. It will be at the top for an upward candlestick and at the bottom for a downward one. The candlestick above shows an upward candlestick.

The candlestick's direction is interpreted using the color of the candlestick or the wide vertical line in particular. An upward candlestick is represented by the color green (as the one above) and red is the color of a downward candlestick. However, please bear in mind that the colors of candlesticks can be customized.

The range of the candlestick is represented by the top and bottom of the wicks (the thin vertical line). It is calculated by subtracting the bottom from the top.

The chart above shows a higher closing price than opening price.

- Doji

The doji (above) illustrates a case where the opening and closing price is the same.

- Line chart.

The bar and candlestick charts are more popularly used than the line chart which only indicates a rough closing or mid-price.

Up Trends – This type of trend is identified when the price is sloping up and the low is getting increasingly higher.

Down Trends – When the price is sloping down and the high is getting increasingly lower, this indicates a down trend.

Support – Price will often fall into a small trading range of channel. It usually drops to a particular lower price level that has been seen before. If you draw a horizontal line by connecting the low from left to right across the chart, the more times the line touches the low, the stronger the support line is said to be. In other words, the price is likely to rise again.

Resistance – When the price begins to rise, it usually goes to the next level that has been seen before. The times the price reaches this high and does not break this line, the more likely it will begin to go back down.

Once the levels of support and resistance are broken, they become the opposite of what they were before, i.e. broken support will become resistance and broken resistance will become support.

The ability to read charts will strengthen your timing strategy for the entry and exit of a trade. In order to increase the chances of maximizing profit, you will need to analyze the charts to see if the market is moving, or is going to move, in the desired direction before entering a trade.

Money Management

Any trading strategy requires an adequate method of managing money in order to be successful. Money management techniques address how much money should be invested at a particular time, as well as how much risk you are willing to take. If you do not follow good money management practice, you will not have any money with which to trade!

Do not risk more than 2% on each trade. The #1 rule is to always ensure that no more than 2% of your invested capital is at risk. For example, the risk on an investment of $1,000 would be limited to $20. If your entry point has been identified as $4 and exit point at $3.80, $0.02 of each stock is at risk. You know that you can risk a total of $20 and $0.02 per share, so you can then find the number of shares that you can invest: $20/$0.02 = 1000 shares. You can purchase 1,000 shares and invest $1,000 * $4 = $4,000 in total for the trade.

Use Stop Losses – Setting stops is an important method of protection for traders. It can prevent a small loss from becoming one of catastrophic proportions. By setting stop losses when entering a trade, you have the opportunity to objectively set your stops from the very beginning.

You have two options when it comes to using stop losses:

1. You can decide to set your stop at a certain percentage of capital that you are willing to lose. Publisher of *Investor's Business Daily* and renowned trader, William O'Neil, recommends setting an amount of 8% per trade.

2. The other option is to use technical analysis to come up with stop loss levels instead of applying an arbitrary percentage.

Whichever option you choose, you definitely do not want to set your stop too close and end up being stopped out of your trade as a result of normal fluctuations in the market. In addition, never second guess your stops and change them when the market fluctuates. They are set at a time when you are most objective and any subsequent market movements can make you lose that objectivity and change the stop loss in a way that you will regret.

If you are using an automated trading software such as the Cooltrade platform, you can easily set the program to avoid losses past a certain point, and seek new alternatives to purchase. This way you can effortlessly regain any potential losses while only needing to give minimal inputs to your funds.

Diversification – Another very important tip for money management is diversification. Good risk management involves ensuring that not all of your money goes towards trades that have the same types of risks. By finding trades with varying risk levels and risk factors, only a proportion of your portfolio will be affected if a single sector experiences a sudden downturn in the market.

Trade with funds you can afford to lose – It is common as a new trader to make the fatal mistake of trading with money that you cannot afford to lose. This scenario is a familiar horror story.

Traders have gone into the market with money that was earmarked for food, medical bills, mortgage and other loan payments and gas among other things. Actions of this type lack common sense. Simply do not trade with money that you cannot afford to lose.

If you are trading using personal funds ask yourself the questions: "Will I be able to pay all of my bills if I lose this money?" and "How would I feel if I lost all of this money?"

If you are trading for a client a similar question to ask yourself is: "How will I feel if I lose all of my client's money?" Now this latter question is not intended to make you panic, but it is just meant to emphasize the importance of recognizing that there is a chance that all funds used can be lost. Therefore, all trades should be made with this thought in mind – but with a clear head and emotional detachment.

Do not trade without a reason – Believe it or not, traders commonly make a trade without knowing the reason why they have made that move. When this happens, they cannot possibly have an exit strategy. This situation leaves the trader entirely without direction, which can only result in the loss of capital. A trader should always know as much information as possible about the stock that is being traded, including the sector within which it falls and its current trading environment.

Test money management skills – A useful way to test your money management skills and trading plan is to carry out simulation trading. By paper trading before investing real money in the market, you can work out any kinks in your money management techniques and trading strategy.

There are many tools available that can automatically track gains and losses of your pretend shares online. One potential method is utilizing Google Finance. You can quickly and easily create a "portfolio" by entering a stock symbol, purchase price, and amount of shares purchased.

Every time you are using your computer, you're only a short search away from the Google Finance webpage which can inform you in a simple format how much you have gained or lost with your chosen shares. If you choose to try a different set of companies to try an improved strategy, you only need to delete your shares and add the new ones.

This Google Finance method is a very simplified tool, and you may feel the need to obtain a different type of software. There are a number of free programs that can maintain this for you, you only need to search and compare to choose one that works best for you.

Practice Discipline – Any money management plan requires discipline. Many investors are quick to enter into an investment and are then at a loss as to what to do next. A money management plan will help to build discipline in investors and prevent the spiraling of emotions, fear and greed that can rear their ugly heads.

Risk Tolerance – Ensure that you thoroughly research all of your possible markets of entry. The markets that you are trading in should fit with your account size and level of risk tolerance.

Avoid taking on too much – In terms of risk, you should always feel comfortable with its level on any given position. If you find that you cannot sleep at night because you are worrying about the previous days' trades, then you are probably in trouble! It means that you are taking on too much risk in your trading portfolio. Therefore, you should stick only to trading positions that you feel comfortable with and try to keep trades to a manageable size in comparison to the overall size of your account.

Trading Plan / Strategy - Successful trading requires the vital element of money management. Therefore, money management should be included as part of the trading strategy. By incorporating money management techniques into your plan, you are accepting that nobody can win 100% of the time and that even the most experienced traders sometimes make mistakes. Money management involves accepting that you may be wrong and having a plan to rectify any mistakes before the losses become too large.

Analyze yourself – Sometimes risky behavior is practiced by individuals as a form of escape or as a substitute for something meaningful that is missing in a person's life. If you find that you refuse to use adequate money management techniques or seem to forget to make a trading plan, it may be time to look at your own personal motivations. Instead of losing all your money because you did not have a good understanding of your subconscious intentions, try to figure it all out and deal with it now. It is necessary to remove all existing barriers to the practice of proper money management techniques so that you can reap all of the possible rewards of trading.

Resist greed – Further to the tip above, greed has resulted in the downfall of both experienced and inexperienced traders alike. It leads to possibly fatal trading errors, including overtrading, taking too much risk and not taking profits when they are at appropriate levels. A way to avoid the emotional trap of greed is to build appropriate safeguards into your trading plan. Once this is done, you can work on maintaining the discipline necessary to follow your trading plan.

Use the abovementioned money management techniques to become a successful trader. Remember if you are not able to hold onto money, then you will not have any funds to trade on the market.

Four Reasons to Invest in Shares

1. The growth rate of the Australian share market has been an average of 12% per year, according to the Australian Stock Exchange. Though the value of shares fluctuates constantly, marked by occasional bursts and booms, buying quality shares with a long-term view is a solid investment.

2. Shares are easy to buy and sell, which makes them a versatile element of your portfolio.

3. The spread of risk is simple because you can hold shares of multiple companies in several regions.

4. Shares require no physical maintenance or insurance.

Types of Shares

There are many different types of shares that a company can make available for sale.

Ordinary Shares

Ordinary shares are the most commonly traded shares. Generally, when people talk about owning shares in a company, they are talking about owning ordinary shares. This is also usually what is referred to when people talk about share prices. In addition to what has already been discussed in the previous section, ordinary shares can have other bonuses attached to them, such as voting rights.

Preference Shares

Different countries have different rules regarding preference shares and availability tends to vary from stock exchange to stock exchange, depending on location. They are a special class of share that are not as common as ordinary shares and also possess features that ordinary shares do not. You will need to do some additional research as to what features are attached to the shares that you are intending to purchase. If in doubt, you should seek advice from your stockbroker, accountant or other financial professional before making a purchase.

Some of these features may include any or all of the following:

- Preferential dividend payments.

This means that if or when dividend payments are made, they are paid to holders of preference shares before the holders of ordinary shares as preference shares have a higher priority for payments.

- Preferential payment in the event of company liquidation.

If the company in which the shares are held goes bankrupt, preferential shareholders are entitled to a share of the assets of the company. However, other debtors including banks and people who work for the company will get paid before preferential shareholders will.

- Preference shares can be convertible.

Some preference shares can be converted to ordinary shares in certain circumstances

- Preference shares may or may not have voting rights attached to them

There are many other features that can be attached to preference shares and your stockbroker will be able to inform you as to what, if any, these may be.

An important note regarding "Penny" stocks or shares

One term that you will come across is *Penny Stocks* or *Penny Shares,* as they can be known. These are shares that meet a certain set of criteria and are traded at a low price per share. The price and criteria once again differ from country to country and sometimes there are also specific rules and regulations which must be followed when they are bought or sold.

Penny shares are mentioned here because it will not take an investor too long to realize that lower priced stock may offer greater benefits over higher priced ones, if they are bought cheaply enough – with the expectation of a significant move in the share price.

Whilst this is true – and a share that is priced at five cents, pence – or whatever the value of your local currency may be, it only has to move to ten cents for you to double your money, minus your commission fees. In most cases, these shares can be considered a highly speculative investment at best. The penny share market is highly volatile and although the price can rise – an investor must remember that it can also fall. At five cents per share, each cent represents a 20% segment of your investment and losses can be significant – but respectively, so can the gains.

The subject of penny shares is a lengthy one and at this level, the markets can be – and have been - manipulated. There are certain hazards that you should be aware of and once again, they are outside the scope of this article. It is therefore strongly recommended that you should see the advice of a financial professional before trading.

In addition to shares, there are many other types of products and services that can be traded on markets and you will no doubt come across a countless variety of other terms when you are researching and trading. These will include options, warranties, futures and commodities, which can be traded on separate markets.

Commodities

The commodities market represents the trade of raw or refined goods and materials. Soft commodities are generally made up of crops and agricultural end products such as coffee, cocoa, fruit and sugar. Hard commodities include mined products such as oil, gold and silver.

The prices that are used in commodities markets are global standard prices – so the price of a barrel of crude oil in the United States is the same as a price of a barrel of crude oil in Australia – at any given time over a 24 hour period.

Many trillions of dollars are invested into the global commodities markets each year and they can offer a very good return on investment. We are all very aware about how the price of oil and gold has risen over the past few years.

Options

Options are contracts that give the purchaser the right, although they remain under no obligation, to buy or sell a share or other asset at a fixed price, either on or before a set date. Certain rules may apply to options depending on location and investors would need to check on local guidelines and requirements.

There are two main types of options where the right to buy is known as a "call" option and the right to sell is known as a "put" option and a simplified example of how this works – ignoring any transaction fees or other associated costs apart from the example premium – follows.

- Example of a Call option.

The current price of a share in ABC Company is $100 per share.

An investor believes that the value of the share will go up over the period of the next three months and wants to invest $10,000. Purchasing the shares directly would enable the investor to obtain 100 shares.

However, by making use of a "call" option, the investor would be able to buy a call contract for 100 shares, by paying an agreed premium of – for the sake of the example – $10 per share on a "strike" price of $150 per share. The total cost of this would be $1,000.

Incidentally, the strike price is the price that the shares must reach, if the entire transaction is to be completed, or exercised, in favour of the investor and it can be higher or lower. The strike price is negotiated when the call contract is purchased and this will directly affect the premium. Further examples on how this work are included below.

Returning to the example, this leaves the investor $9,000 to either invest separately, or to retain.

Three months later, again for the sake of the example, the price of the share rises to $150.

The investor may now buy the 100 shares at the initially agreed price of $100 per share, thus realizing an immediate profit of $40 per share ($150 Current Price – $100 Initial Price – $10 Premium) for a total profit of $4,000 less expenses.

If, after the three month period, the share price did not go up to $150 per share, the entire contract would be void and the investor would lose the $1,000 paid for the contract.

A brief example of the variable premiums would be as follows. These premiums do not reflect the actual premiums on transactions of this size. They are just meant to demonstrate that there is a relation between the strike rate and the premium – and the relation is that the higher the strike rate from the initial price, the less the premium. This is due to the fact that there is less chance of the strike rate being achieved.

Call contract with an initial price of $100 and a strike price of $130. Premium $15

Call contract with an initial price of $100 and a strike price of $150. Premium $10

Call contract with an initial price of $100 and a strike price of $180. Premium $5

- Example of a Put Option.

A Put option works in the opposite way to a call option and gives an investor who believes that the price of a certain stock will go down over a period of time – the option to sell the stock at a certain price.

A Put Buyer is an investor or trader who buys the put option and the Put Writer is a trader who sells the option.

Following the rules of the call option example above, the current price of a share in ABC Company is $100 per share.

An investor who believes that the value of the share will go down over the period of the next three months, purchases a put contract from a Put Writer for 100 shares, by paying an agreed premium of – for the sake of the example – $10 per share on a "strike" price of $70. Again, the total cost for this would be $1,000 and again, this leaves the investor $9,000.

Three months later, the investor has once again speculated correctly and the price of the share indeed falls to $70.

The investor exercises the option and buys the shares at the current price of $70 per share, selling them to the Put Writer for $100 per share, thus making a profit of $20 per share. ($100 Initial Price – $70 Current Price – $10 Premium)

If the strike price did not drop to $70 or below, the investor would lose the premium of $1,000.

Options hold various advantages over the ownership of ordinary shares.

First, by purchasing a premium at a fraction of the cost of the actual share itself, an investor has much more buying power – or leverage, as it is known. If, for example, the premium was 10% of the actual purchase price the investor would be able to use the remaining 90% of their funds to purchase additional options leaving the possibility of a larger profit upon successful execution – than would have been possible if the shares were purchased themselves.

Secondly, if an investor did not want to utilize the remaining funds, they can be kept safely in a bank. Alternatively, using diversification, you could buy options in ten different market sectors. Of course, there are no guarantees that all or any of the options purchased may reach the striking price, in which case the entire investment is lost.

Thirdly, the rewards for investment are much higher, but the risk will reflect this.

The main disadvantage with options is that they are purely speculative. By owning the shares themselves, at the very least, an investor is highly likely to have something to fall back on – in the event of a slump in prices. With options, if the strike price is not achieved, the contract is worthless and the premium paid is lost.

Another disadvantage is that options are not available across all shares and all markets. In addition, they are quite complicated for beginners.

By researching on the Internet, you will find many pages of information and tutorials regarding options and your stockbroker can give you advice and assistance with regard to their purchase.

An important note regarding Binary Options

Over the past few years, you may have seen adverts posted in pages around the internet – for sites that trade in Binary Options. These are known as Binary Option Trading Platforms and although they can be considered extremely easy to use, they can also – if used in the wrong way – be addictive in the same way as gambling and gaming sites, so care must be taken when using them.

Although the following should be taken as an extremely oversimplified explanation – they work in a similar way to options. In contrast, the user is in control of most of the aspects of the trade, such as the amount of money that is used in the bid and the amount of time until the trade expires – which can be as little as five minutes.

In essence, Binary Options provide a way to bet on whether a price in a given field will go up or down over a certain amount of time. If you predict correctly, you win your bid/stake plus a bonus percentage that was displayed to you before you initiated the transaction. If you predict incorrectly, you lose your bid/stake.

Again, it is recommended that you seek the advice of a professional before attempting to use a site of this nature.

About Market Sectors

If you take a look at any daily financial paper, you'll notice that certain shares are grouped together into sections. In the same way, as has already been briefly mentioned, stock exchanges list the shares that are traded on their trading floors, into groups – or sectors. A couple of advantages of this are that analysts and investors can see, at a glance, how one industry is competing against a similar industry in the same sector. A second advantage is that a complete section can be compared directly against another.

Broadly speaking, a sector is a subsection of the market and these sectors may be further divided into sub-sectors, although the classifications can vary from stock market to stock market.

Generally, they are divided into industrial and resource companies with Resource sectors being made up of Energy and Minerals, whilst the Industrial sectors constitute a mix of all other streams including banking and insurance, newspapers and media, telecommunications and retail companies.

Trends

Being able to understand trends is an essential part of being a trader. The KISS ("Keep it simple, stupid") principle tells us that we do not need to develop any trading methodologies that are too complicated. A simple strategy that involves trend analysis is all it takes for success. After all, financial trading is certainly not brain surgery!

Following trends to make trades is very different than the common "buy and hold" strategy that is often touted. Once trends begin, a trader can enter the market, and if the trend shows signs of deterioration, that is a signal to exit the market.

Following trends for trading requires great discipline and emotional detachment. It involves staying with the trading strategy through the invariable ups and downs of the market. The aim is to ride on, or capture, the majority of a market trend (whether upwards or downwards) in order to make a profit. This ride may take a trader on an uncomfortable journey of market volatility.

Not all volatility is bad. In fact, avoiding volatility may result in an inability to stay with the trend over the long-term. A long-term systematic plan involves patiently riding the wave of volatility and not avoiding it. In this way, a trader is less likely to be forced out of a position while in the middle of a major move in the long-run.

Trading using trends assists in making the decision of how to initiate trades. Successful traders follow trends and always trade in the same direction as the recent price movement. All traders have the tools to find and follow trends. Winning traders also wait until a trend has been confirmed before taking a position that is in line with that trend.

A major advantage of following trends is that it means that as a trader you will never miss any of the market's major moves. If the market you are interested in starts moving upward, having turned from a downwards direction, the signal is to "buy".

For at least the past thirty years, following trends has been a style of trading that has been practiced with a high measure of success. Following trends is statistically valid because traders have tested it for years and years. Trends will always exist and they can be profitably traded up and down.

The world will be constantly changing and the beginning or end of a trend cannot be predicted. Trends are like the weather; they can be very unpredictable. However, a sound trading strategy will seek to take advantage of market changes, as indicated by trends, in order to make a profit.

Following trends is premised on good business principles. The dynamic environment will not hurt you as a trader if your principles are designed to adapt. Being able to adapt is the key to making money from the market by following trends.

Many supporters of trends liken them to epidemics. An epidemic can start with just a few people, but then quickly spread through the population as it multiplies. Similarly, market trends can begin out of nowhere and move in either direction, i.e. up or down. They can quickly progress and present the opportunity for large profits if the trend was traded.

Likening a trend to an epidemic is not easily grasped by all traders. It is sometimes difficult to understand because the end result is often not proportionate to the cause.

Some traders fall into the trap of wanting to understand the trend and fail to take advantage of the opportunity presented by the trade. Instead of using it to win, they are obsessed with being right.

Proportionality in market trends cannot be expected by traders. It is possible that small events can lead to huge market changes which may occur very quickly. In this way, trends can be powerfully rewarding. Historically, traders that follow trends experience a significantly higher profit per trade than loss per trade.

Following trends must always involve a plan. There is no room for wild guesses and emotional upheaval; it requires a high level of self-discipline to follow precise trading strategies and rules.

There is also a disadvantage associated with following trends. Indicators are unable to determine whether the profitable move of the market is one for the short-term or a move for the long-run.

It may happen quite often that traders who follow trends get caught as signals immediately turn against their position and cause small losses. Multiple small losses of this kind can become quite substantial and lead to the temptation to abandon the strategy altogether.

Can you follow a trend? Let's keep it simple. Imagine the stability of the market represented by a straight line. The line can remain as it is, begin to go down or start to rise. When there is no movement, we can safely do nothing. However, when the line starts to go down, we need to be ready to exit at that point and remove any cash. If the line beings to rise, that is a signal that we can now re-enter the market.

We have already discussed momentum. You need to invest only in those markets that are experiencing the most momentum. Follow the trends for as long as possible and use money management techniques, such as stop losses. Based on adequate analysis of trends, you should be able to determine whether a downward trend is likely to correct itself or if it is an indication of a longer-term reversal.

You may be asking the question: "How do I know when a trend exists?" There are various technical tools that can signal a trend, but there are also a great number of false signals as well. There can only be three types of trends: up, down or flat. It is also possible to refer to trends between any two points located on a price chart.

A trader can draw a moving average on two randomly chosen points on a chart. The pattern that arises as a result can be analyzed as a trend. In this way, it becomes necessary to have a basic knowledge of the economic factors that can cause trends before deciding whether a chart pattern is valid.

It is possible to attain this understanding of economic factors responsible for trends. All you have to do is familiarize yourself with the bigger picture of the market, understand what motivates market participants and recognize the various stages of the business cycle.

KISS is a term coined by Kelly Johnson, a leading engineer. He gave his design team a set of tools and challenged them to create a jet aircraft which was repairable using only the tools of an average mechanic in the field under combat decisions.

The KISS principle highlights that the simplest solution should be used to deal with a situation.

With the KISS approach, it is not necessary for you to be the smartest person in the room in order to be successful. In fact, you do not want to be too clever. If you notice that the markets are going down, the action you are to take is to simply get out. There is nothing more that needs to be done other than watch and wait to reinvest.

Secret to Long-Term Gains

Now you know all about the KISS principle and why it is necessary to "keep it simple, stupid". Consistency is also another pre-requisite to achieve long-term gains while trading. The following are some simple tips to follow to ensure that you make a consistent income as a trader:

- *Research.* Read widely in order to understand the workings of the stock market and its trends, as well as the economic conditions around the globe. Learning from the experiences of other successful traders is another way to prepare yourself to make your own investments.

- *Manage your financials.* How to manage your money is a key element of trading. If you do not know how to hold onto your money, you will not have any to invest.

- *Think long-term.* You should trade with the long-term in mind. Although speculation may be a part of your portfolio, there are likely to be stocks that do appreciate in value over time and you will want to take advantage of those.

- *Do not panic.* Volatility is common within the market. You need to hold onto your emotions and let logic lead the way. The only consistent thing that emotional trading will lead to is consistent losses – not profits.

- *Willing to take a loss.* Do not refuse to take a loss. This attitude is one of the more common reasons for failure by traders. A lack of a defined exit point when a trade is carried out usually leads to this failure. A trader should always know where and when he/she will get out if they are found to be wrong.

- *Diversify.* We will speak more about this later in this book. By creating and maintaining a portfolio with various stocks, the portfolio will be a diversified one that spreads, and therefore minimizes, your risk.

- *Courage and Persistence.* The traits of courage and persistence that are needed by a trader are best explained by stalwarts Theodore Roosevelt and Calvin Coolidge. They seem strikingly appropriate for all traders committed to the endless quest of trading profits in the market. These statements can be regularly reviewed for motivation.

  Courage: *"The credit belongs to the man who is actually in the arena, who strives valiantly; who knows the great enthusiasms, the great devotions, and spends himself in a worthy cause; who at best, knows*

the triumph of high achievement; and who, at the worst, if he fails, at least fails while daring greatly, so that his place shall never be with those cold and timid souls who know neither victory nor defeat."
~ Theodore Roosevelt

Persistence: *"Nothing in the world can take the place of persistence. Talent will not; nothing is more common than unsuccessful men with talent. Genius will not; unrewarded genius is almost a proverb. Education will not; the world is full of educated derelicts. Persistence and determination alone are omnipotent".*
~Calvin Coolidge

- *Hard work and Practice.* Notwithstanding the other tips above, hard work and practice may be the most important advice for a successful trader. Natural talent has not proven to provide traders with great success. However, tedious and painstaking hard work and practice has resulted in profitable trades and traders who continue to be successful in the market.

As with any profession, consistent practice and hard work are the keys to rise to the top. There are so many facets of trading: including a wealth of data, various analyses, alternative strategies, etc. A trader needs to be able to get a handle on each of these aspects and to do so and become successful requires a lot of hard work.

A trader can get a better grip on the various facets of trading by practicing. Practical knowledge provides more value than any theoretical perspective. Practice can offer great levels of insight into, and experience with, the market.

Reading from books, articles and magazines are beneficial to learn the theory. However, knowledge of theory is not enough to achieve great levels of success on a daily basis.

Learning does not have an end. To be continuously successful, a trader will have to keep on learning and improving on his/her skills. The pace of learning will vary between individuals. Some traders may learn fast in the beginning and then slow down until they feel they have absorbed all they need to know. Other traders may learn at a slower pace and then acquire more and more practical knowledge as time goes on. But regardless of a trader's learning curve, the best traders will be those who make a concerted effort to keep on learning and work hard to meet the demand for learning.

There are those people that may believe that there are individuals that are simply born to succeed at trading. However, a natural gift in this regard does not really exist. Greatness can only be achieved through years of hard work. Just as nobody is born a CEO, nobody is born a successful trader. High-level performance cannot be based on natural gifts without hard work and practice being a part of the equation.

Talent in trading does not refer to levels of intelligence, motivation or other personality traits. Instead it refers to an individual's ability to do certain things or deal with specific issues very well.

The best traders are those who dedicate hours to practicing trades. In this way, they are able to better their understanding of the market and improve their trading performance. Consistent practice is a crucial element of success.

You may argue that some things cannot be practiced, and you would be correct. For instance, trading involves making judgments and decisions with imperfect information under conditions of uncertainty, through interaction with people and by searching for information. These things cannot be truly practiced. However, the attitude to work can be practiced and this mindset can be used to carry out these activities in your daily work.

Undergoing a shift in attitude may not be easy. It may require fundamental change in the way the market is viewed. But practice will ensure that a trader gets better and better at it.

Long-term gains are what every trader should aim for. Simplicity and consistency is the secret to profits over time. So always remember your KISS principle and my tips for consistency when planning your trading strategy as well as when you are carrying out your trades.

Sector Analysis

A trader can benefit from stock analysis or focusing on groups of stocks that perform the same service or produce the same goods. Sectors can be divided into basic materials, conglomerates, financial, medical care, services, technology, utilities, consumer goods and industrial goods. Each of these sectors can be further divided into sub-sectors.

Sector analysis is useful because stocks within the same sector usually behave in the same way. If one stock indicates a bearish trend, the others in the same sector will more than likely show the same tendency. Similarly, if a stock within a sector shows a bullish tendency, the other stocks within that sector will behave in the same manner.

Stocks within a particular sector will follow the same pattern because market and economic conditions will affect companies within the same industry in similar ways. By understanding the movement of stocks within sectors, a trader will have an entry point for a better trade.

When stocks are further broken down into subsectors, a trader can delve deeper into the sector and come up with some tighter analysis. Better trades can result from zooming in on a smaller group of similar stocks.

An example is Walmart, which is a part of the Food and Staples Retail sector and can also be further placed in the Hypermarkets and Super Centers subsector.

Other companies within the same sub-sector include PriceSmart, BJs Wholesale Club and Costco. The stocks within this subsector have many similarities, because they are affected by the same variables.

For instance, a rise in the price of gasoline will affect each company in the subsector because of the increased cost of delivering products. In addition, a robust economy during the holidays will lead to bullish tendencies for each company.

Sector analysis can be used by traders who are practicing a top-down approach to stock selection. With this method, the most promising sectors are identified followed by the identification of the individual stocks to be bought.

This type of analysis can also be used by traders who are implementing a sector-rotation strategy, which essentially involves shifting assets between sectors. Not all sectors will be strong all at the same time, so a trader is able to move money and make better trades on the sectors that are strong. A trader who is following momentum will focus on the market leaders. A useful strategy is to pursue the stocks that are moving the most in order to earn the most profit.

An alternative to dealing with only one stock is to purchase a fund that includes various stocks from one sector. However, depending on the conditions within the economy at any given time, these exchange traded funds or mutual funds will usually either do extremely well or poorly.

Sector analysis can be used by traders to quickly find trading opportunities in stocks within a particular sector. This search can be facilitated by several sector indexes, which represent a basket of the various securities that are associated with a given sector, for example, the Biotechnology Index.

Using this index, several stocks should be found in that sector that have similar price patterns. A trader can focus on the opportunities presented by analyzing sector indexes.

The measurement of relative strengths and weaknesses can be carried out using sector analysis as a benchmark. Within any sector index, there will be some securities that will under-perform the index and some that will outperform it. This phenomenon is natural as you will always have the leaders in the pack as well as those that lag behind.

Using relative strength analysis, the performance of individual securities can be evaluated within a particular sector by comparing them to their sector index. By doing this, a trader can determine which patterns show the best chances of a successful trade.

Financial author, Stan Weinstein, in his book *Secrets for Profiting in Bull and Bear Markets* usefully sums up the importance of sector analysis. Following market risk, sector performance is described as the most influential factor affecting stock performance (otherwise known as sector risk). Weinstein's recommendation is that a trader:

1.   Determine the direction of the market;

2.   Choose the sectors which are performing the best; and

3.   Select the best performing stocks from those sectors identified above.

The only additional recommendation that I would add to this list is to determine the health of the economy overall before analyzing sectors and choosing the ones with most growth potential.

Picking the right sector also involves looking at various timeframes. By looking at two or more time frames, you will be able to choose the sectors that are performing well currently and which have shown strength over a longer time period. The time frames being analyzed will differ between persons and will be dependent on their overall time frame.

The strength of a security and the market index can be compared using the Relative Strength Comparison (RSC). It compares the price change of a security with a benchmark security.

The RSC can be undertaken and plotted on a chart in order to interpret the line as follows:

- The security is performing better than base security if the RSC is rising.

- Sideways movements mean that both securities are showing the same level of performance.

- The security is performing worse than the base security if the RSC is decreasing.

The sector that is at or near the top of the list for highest performing sectors will be chosen. If some diversity is needed, the top two or three sectors can be picked.

The process for finding the best individual stocks is similar to that of finding the right market. Multiple timeframes should be looked at to ensure that there is a history of the stock moving well. The stocks to be bought for your portfolio should be those that have performed the best during two or three timeframes.

In order to carry out Weinstein's recommendations, a sectors comparison chart is a handy tool. It provides the trader with a general overview of the relative performance of different sectors (e.g. utilities, property trusts, information technology and health care).

Another useful tool is a sector watch list. It compares the major component stocks with the sector index.

The entire stock market is too much for a trader to focus on all at one time. Therefore, a more successful strategy involves sector analysis and concentrating on one group of stocks at a time. The stocks within a particular sector will generally move together, subject to one or two exceptions, because the market leaders will be affected by the same economic conditions.

Why Invest in Shares/Equities

We have already discussed a few of the advantages of investing in Shares, or Equities, and we can now take a look at this subject in more detail.

Whilst it is true that investing in shares can sometimes be risky, if done responsibly, with care and research over the long term, shares can offer a very good return on investment capital that can outperform bonds that in fairness, carry a much lower risk – property investments.

Most shares will provide a bi–annual dividend payment, if the company is profitable, that can then be reinvested or placed into a bank account. Shares in these companies are known as Income Stocks – since they provide a regular source of income.

Often, when a company is fairly new, it may not pay dividends on its shares at all, choosing instead to reinvest any profits back into the business. In this case, the share price can steadily grow and then, when the company is more established, the shares may begin to return dividends – although at times, some very established companies will reinvest their profits as well.

Shares in these companies are known as Growth Stocks and there are a number of things that an investor can look for when selecting these shares, such as a history of strong earnings, strong forward earning growth, stable and relative costs when compared to revenue and a stable or increased return on investment.

Although not very common, highly publicized privatizations of either government run or state owned companies and their respective Initial Public Offers can provide investors with some of the best opportunities to buy short term Growth Stock, since the shares are usually offered for tender or sale at a discounted price, before the first day of trading. Depending on how high profile the company is, some of these offers can be oversubscribed, but, if you manage to purchase shares using this method, then you can make some extremely good capital gains over the short term as there is very often an extremely active trading period following the launch.

The choice of investment direction is down to the individual investor but it is here where diversification comes into play. By splitting your investment capital between income stock and growth stock, in addition to covering different market sectors, you will be in the best possible position to benefit from all of the research that you have done. It is always important to spread your risk – and investing for the long term is usually a more successful overall strategy.

You will be able take further steps to safeguard yourself and limit your losses. By using a stop loss system, you can make use of a trigger that will automatically sell your shares when they drop below a given price. However, once again, this should not lead you to believe that you can become complacent with your portfolio as there are certain circumstances in which the stop loss system may not work and this is mainly to do with market opening and closing times.

For example – if the particular stock market that you use closes and there is a problem with a company in which you hold shares during the night – maybe in a division located in another country, the share price may open at a significantly lower price than that set for your stop loss trigger. Although the trigger will work when your local stock market opens, you will still have lost money and this is why it is important to keep on top of not only the financial news in general, but most importantly, the news regarding the particular companies that constitute the make–up of your particular portfolio.

Since markets tend to move in cycles, the prices constantly fluctuate. Therefore, it must be said that it is important to keep track of your portfolio at all times and you should always be aware of what is happening to the companies in which you hold shares. Rumors of poor trading figures can start quite a while before the actual figures are published. If you are able to keep abreast of the financial news, then you will be in a position to act accordingly. However, if you only check how well your shares are performing on a weekly or monthly basis, then by the time you find out, the damage may have already been done and you will have lost money.

Another important item worthy of note is that the shares in your portfolio are an asset and should be treated as such. You MUST know when to cut your losses if a particular stock is under–performing and you should never get too attached to a share in a particular company. Although markets experience hiccups all the time and certain share prices may drop – and then rally, if you feel that the price won't return to an acceptable level, then you must be prepared to get rid of it. Holding on to a stock in the hope of the price rising, may make you suffer more in the long run.

If you are a complete beginner or a novice and you'd like to know what it's like to trade on the markets – without the risk of losing your money, then you can always use something called a practice trading account.

Most stockbrokers offer these market simulator services online and these accounts will give you an amount of "virtual" money to trade with. You can buy and sell shares in the same way that other traders do – but you have the advantageous safety net of being able to make mistakes as a newcomer. If you lose everything, you simply start over.

It's an excellent way to get valuable market experience that you'll learn from – without having to spend any money. Simply type "practice share trading account" into your favorite search engine and you will be able to find an account to suit what will become your trading style. Be sure to read through all of the terms and conditions if they are present, as some sites offer more facilities than others.

There's a whole host of other information on all of the subjects covered here – that is readily available on the internet. No matter what your level of experience is, you'll always find something new to learn and whilst you're learning, always remember that even the most successful traders – the ones who have made millions at one time or another - have all picked shares that have lost.

In conclusion, if done correctly and with care, trading or investing in shares can offer a highly interesting way to spend your free time and can offer a good return on your money. Again, always seek professional advice if you are unsure about something.

The Difficulty of Diversification

When reviewing individual investment portfolios, I often see individual stocks. Many times the investor tells me that the broker advising him was trying to help him set up his "own mutual fund." In other instances, investors gravitate to individual stocks hoping to find and own the next Microsoft, Yahoo or another company that will hit it big. It's a great thought, but the problem is that individual investors rarely have the resources to become properly diversified on their own. To illustrate, let's look at a simple example:

Let's say I want to get completely diversified in the largest U.S. companies—the S&P 500. If I want to own all 500 stocks, the first thing I would consider is how to buy them as inexpensively as possible. This would necessitate buying them in "round lots," or one hundred share units. Trading in smaller units, or "odd lots," is more expensive. Let's assume that the average share price is $50 dollars. Based on these numbers, the amount of money I would have to invest would be:

> 500 companies x $50 per share x 100 share units = $2.5 million dollars

This amount would allow for diversification in the area of large blend stocks. Now we have to consider large value stocks, small blend stocks, small value stocks, international large, international small, etc. Obviously, most investors would have a hard time coming up with the first $2.5 million dollars, let alone the substantial amount of money needed to cover the other categories. The bottom line is that this type of investing is simply not feasible for the average individual investor.

What is a Commingled Investment Vehicle?

So, if we can't safely diversify on our own without having millions in capital, what choice do we individual investors have? One solution is a commingled investment vehicle. A commingled investment vehicle is just a fancy term for an investment product that is the result of pooling multiple investors' assets. It's like throwing a slew of different items in a single bucket of which a large group of people all have ownership. Common examples of commingled investment vehicles are:

- Mutual Funds

- Variable Annuity Sub-accounts

- Exchange Traded Funds (ETFs)

By pooling our assets with other investors, we can achieve much higher levels of diversification than we can on our own, and everyone who owns the commingled vehicle will own the assets in the same exact proportions. This type of investing also allows the individual investor to take advantage of the thousands of stocks (in the United States alone) from which we have to choose. If we look at the cost of owning all of them, we can easily see why commingling is such a popular concept.

Unsystematic Risk. The primary risk that commingled investment vehicles are designed to alleviate is unsystematic risk. Unsystematic risk is the risk of loss that comes with investing in an insufficient number of different investment vehicles. For example, there is a much greater likelihood that one large AUS company could go bankrupt than there is that all large AUS companies would go out of business. There is also a greater level of volatility with individual stocks that we don't see with the market as a whole. Since we are not expected to gain any additional return from taking this risk, it makes little sense to subject ourselves to it.

The graph below shows the volatility of individual stocks versus the market at large. The areas shaded with yellow show the greater swings in value that individual stocks are often subject to, while the market as a whole tends to stay within a more controlled range of returns. This graph helps explain another term used to describe what is known as uncompensated risk. Quite simply, we shouldn't take risks that we're not paid to take.

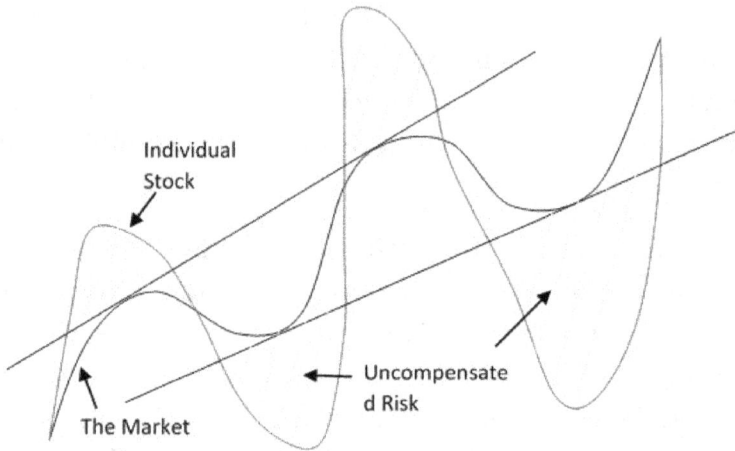

Individual Stock

Uncompensated Risk

The Market

Diversification or "Diworseification"

Diversification is a portfolio management technique that is always touted for reducing investment risk. However, over-diversification or "diworseification" can be a harmful thing.

The term "diworseification" is said to have been coined both by famed investor, Warren Buffet, and well-known investment author, Peter Lynch, in his book *One Up on Wall Street*. Whatever the origin, it was initially used to describe the company specific problem of owning too many investments. The term is now often used to describe inefficient diversification with regard to an investment portfolio, which then removes any risk reduction gained from diversifying.

The top financial analysts all recommend that investors "Diversify! Diversify! Diversify!" to reduce risk. However, in today's trading environment, diversification often becomes "diworseification".

Too much diversification can result in your portfolio being crippled so that you are prevented from making significant positive returns on your investment.

The more positions you add, essentially the more you are increasing your risk and reducing the likelihood of earning a substantial return on your winners.

Due to the fact that the chance is low that all of the stocks you pick will in actuality be winners, it is a better strategy to allocate most of your money to a few of the top performing stocks that are at a proper buying point as opposed to purchasing various stocks simply hoping that they will turn out to be winners.

It is far easier to pick a couple winners than to pick 15 or 20 winning stocks. Buying additional stocks is unnecessary. Alternatively, you can continue to add to the couple of winning stocks you already have and seek opportunities arising from key support levels.

You can begin conservatively and buy a small amount at first. If the stock seems to perform consistently well, you can then add to it to maximize your profits. More importantly, if its performance deteriorates, you need to sell it to minimize your losses.

A good trader will often follow over thirty markets on as many as three different time frames. This strategy is followed because a market may only trend about 30% of the time, which means that the majority of the time a market is choppy and is not trending. In order to compensate for the time a market is not trending, a successful trader will follow many markets in order to have a better chance of finding existing trends. Differing time frames afford a trader the benefit from studying the varied ways of the setup of a trend and how it is followed through each time.

At times, a trade will rocket upwards very quickly and drop downwards even faster, which is good for short-term trades. Other times you will see a profitable trade slowly rising and then falling, which is beneficial for the long-term.

A trading system should have the ability to follow various markets since any one individual market may afford profitable trading opportunities at any given time. If markets tend to only trend approximately one third of the time, it is more time efficient to follow multiple markets at the same time.

When discussing diversification, we cannot leave out market sectors. For instance, there are multiple market sectors in the commodities markets. Each market sector has even more markets. These market sectors may include fuels, meats, metals and grains.

Looking at grains in particular, there are three major markets within that sector: wheat, corn and soybeans. Other markets include oats and rice. Certain grains even have different variations. For instances, soybeans can be broken down further into soybeans, soybean meal and soybean oil. Similarly wheat trades include winter wheat and spring wheat. The greater the number of markets you can follow as a trader, the greater the level of diversification you will experience.

With more market sectors being applied to your portfolio, the likelihood of catching trending trades increases exponentially. A good trading system is especially handy in these cases; you will be able to easily calculate trends across various market sectors.

Diversification with regard to time frames is also important. There will be times when trades within the short-term time frame will perform the best, and there are other times when the medium-term and long-term time frames will do better. The combination and application of these three different time frames in your portfolio will result in a more consistent level of performance.

Trading systems can assist in pursuing the aim of diversification. Without a system in place, a trader will find it very hard to follow multiple markets every day. Trade Think is a trading system that can be used to track the markets. It is able to perform numerous calculations on many markets with lightning speed and it can do this every single day. Unlike an employee, the trading system will not call in sick!

There will be times when you will want some time for relaxation with family, friends or simply by yourself. At these times, a system good at following diversified trends will by very handy. It will be able to automatically generate trading signals based on multiple markets, market sectors and time frames. A good trading system will assist in leaving the emotion out of trading.

Of course, like most things, there is a catch with this type of trading system. Some traders may find the entry fee unmanageable. It may require as much as $30,000 to follow one time frame on approximately twenty markets over seven different market sectors. To follow twenty markets over three time frames may involve a minimum of $100,000.

What are the signs of "diworseification"?

1. *Investing in too many mutual funds within any one category.* Otherwise investment costs increase; there is greater requirement for investment. Due diligence and the rate of diversification achieved by holding more than one position is reduced.

2. *Too much reliance on multi-manager investments.* These products lack customization, have a high cost and undertake a diluted due diligence.

3. *Owning too many individual stock positions.* An excessive number of individual stock positions can result in onerous due diligence requirements, complicated tax issues and a performance that only imitates a stock index at a higher cost.

4. *Owning non-publicly traded, privately held investments that are similar to publicly traded ones.* In other words, holding private "non-traded" investments that do not differ fundamentally from publicly traded products that you already own. These alternative investments, while aiming to provide increased diversification, may result in an increased investment risk.

When you are practicing the legitimate method of diversification, be careful not to fall into the trap of "diworseification". It will ultimately nullify any attempts at risk reduction through diversification.

Judging your Portfolio

Now that we know the various investment strategies and the criteria for picking the right one for you, we'll discuss how to accurately see how your choices are doing. There are two ways to judge your portfolio's performance. The first method is called the Macro Method of sizing up performance. With the Macro Method, you must look at whether your portfolio performed within expectations as a whole. In other words, look at the return over a calendar year and compare it to the range of returns you expected from the portfolio. You may recall that you can get an idea of what to expect by looking at the standard deviation of the portfolio, and based on that, you can calculate the range of returns that the portfolio might deliver. This is an important tool that allows you to relax during trying economic times.

For example, if you used an Aggressive mix, your expected return is approximately eight percent above inflation after expenses. (If inflation is four percent, then you have a long-term expected return of twelve percent.) Simply calculate the overall range of returns using the gross return (twelve percent in this example) as the base. If your standard deviation were eighteen, then you would expect—with a ninety-five percent level of confidence—that the portfolio won't return more than forty-eight percent [12 + (18 x 2)].

On the down side, you could see a negative twenty-four percent in one year [12 − (18 x 2)]. As long as your portfolio is in between those two numbers (-24 percent and +48 percent), then you know that the portfolio is performing within the range of expectations. A ninety-five percent level of confidence means that only five percent of historical returns would have been outside of these ranges.

The second way to judge performance is to look at each mutual fund and make sure that it matches the return (within reason) of the asset class it attempts to replicate. This is called the Micro Method because it allows you to focus on the smaller picture or "parts" of your portfolio. For instance, you may want to compare the return of your large company U.S. fund to the performance of the S&P 500. If the fund had significant underperformance, there is a problem. Despite what you may think, though, you don't want the fund to over perform significantly either. If the S&P 500 goes down ten percent and the fund goes up ten percent, then you know that the manager gambled with your money and got lucky. If they can gamble and get lucky, then they can surely gamble and get unlucky.

Some asset classes are easier to replicate with mutual funds (like large U.S. and large international), so this process of benchmarking is not a perfect science. I typically just look at each fund and compare it to its index counterpart. As long as you exercise care in choosing your funds when assembling the portfolio, you won't likely see a great deal of difference between the returns of your funds and their respective indexes (or the asset classes they are tracking).

Here is a list of some of the indexes as a basis of comparison and the asset classes they represent:

- S&P 500 – Large U.S. stocks

- Barra U.S. Large Value (or Russell 1000 Value) – Large U.S. Value stocks

- Russell 2000 – Small U.S. stocks

- Russell 2000 Value – Small U.S. Value stocks

- EAFE Index – International Large stocks

Using the Macro and Micro Methods of judging your portfolio provide a powerful tool for the investor to create peace of mind. Far too often, we are tempted to make changes in our mutual funds when no change is warranted. Using these evaluative methods gives us a "permission slip" to just leave things alone and let market forces do their thing. It gives us confidence that everything is going just as it should and that we don't have to lose sleep over worrying that we made bad choices.

In the end, that confidence will be an important ingredient in your success. Confident investors are disciplined investors, and disciplined investors are successful investors.

Getting Started

You shouldn't go to the grocery store hungry. This simple advice can help save you money, because when you do, you're going to buy based on what you want to eat right that minute (which is everything), and not about what you and your family need for meals. Going to the grocery store involves making a plan, building a list from that plan, and carefully comparing the options on the list.

Making investment decisions is a lot like that. If you rush in, you're going to make reckless decisions designed to make you money now, as opposed to making smart, long-term, forward thinking decisions that can provide for your financial security in the long term. You also probably won't make much money without a solid plan in place.

When you're getting started investing in shares, super funds, or other financial instruments, you need to start by making that plan. This plan contains your answers to five key questions:

- What are my goals?
- When should I start investing?
- How much money should I invest?
- How should I invest it?
- When should I sell?

This chapter will walk you through some ways to begin answering these questions, and give you some things to think about along the way.

Answering these five questions will give you an "investment plan." This plan will help guide you through the investment process. Think about it as a blueprint for building your financial future. Just like the plan for a building, some things might get changed along the way. Sudden, unexpected expenses, unanticipated job loss, or other emergencies might crop up and force you to revise your plan. Similarly, financial windfalls, like inheritances, bonuses, raises, and promotions might encourage you to accelerate your financial goals. Having a plan for what you want your future to look like will help you deal more effectively with those circumstances.

It will also help you make your investment decisions. Knowing what you want out of your money, when you might need it, and how much risk you can tolerate will help you decide a lot of important issues like:

- What instruments you want to use for your investment

- What time frame you want to use for the sale of your investment tools

- How should you distribute the money you invest

- How much money you need

- How much risk can you tolerate

- How involved you want to be with managing each part of your portfolio

- How you will choose your investments

- How you will choose to sell your investments

- What information you will rely on to make your financial decisions

To address these issues and more, you need to form a strong investment plan. To form a strong investment plan, you need to spend some time reflecting on your financial goals and your current situation.

What are my goals?

You probably don't spend a lot of time thinking about your immediate financial goals because they're so short-term. You want to get your next pay check so that you can pay your house note, your car note, your utility bills, your credit cards, and so on. That's fine for the day-to-day, but what about your long-term plans? Do you want to buy a house? What about retiring early? Would you like to take your family on a big vacation? Do you want to someday start your own business?

Money isn't an end in and of itself. It reflects the ability to do something. Maybe you just want to ensure your financial security and the financial security of your family. That's a realistic goal. Maybe you want, instead, to fund personal philanthropic work. You want to endow a scholarship or charitable organization that will "do good" in the world. That's also a realistic goal. Both of these financial goals, though, will require you to have wealth available at a certain time.

Thinking about how much money you need to accomplish these goals is an excellent starting point for building a financial plan. Let's walk through one scenario- you're saving for your retirement. To understand this scenario, let's make a couple of assumptions. These are just meant to show how the math works- these might be very different than your goals.

- You're 40 years old, and want to keep working until you're 65 years old.

- You want a retirement income of $1,000 a week.

- Inflation remains around 3% per year

- Your tax rate stays the same

Those first two assumptions are your goals. In order to achieve them while investing a reasonable amount, say $100 per week, which would give you $5,200 per year. In order to meet your goal of $1000 per week in retirement income, you would need to find a way to generate a 15% return on that investment. There are investment tools available that can deliver that kind of return, but they may involve a considerable amount of risk. Now, since this is your retirement nest egg, you may want to be somewhat risk averse, and so may wish to adjust your savings amount per week up, while looking for lower return/ lower risk options. If you're much younger and hope to retire early, you might look at investment options that offer a higher return, but involve greater risk.

Ultimately, your goals are the most important part of establishing your financial plan. If you know your financial goals and have a clear understanding of what you can afford, there's no reason you can't make plans that will achieve those goals, and reap the rewards of financial success. Once you determine your goals, you will know how hard your money needs to work for you in order to achieve them.

When should I start?

This is a complicated question. A lot of people have serious anxiety about getting involved in investment. They think it's the wrong time to get involved, or they think they don't know enough to make that decision, or they don't think they understand the market well enough to make any progress. Like a lot of important financial decisions, this one depends on your goals.

If you're making short-term investments, then you need to time your purchases and sales to correspond to high levels of market volatility. This is incredibly complicated, and many professionals don't do it right very often. This kind of investment is all about seizing opportunities as they present themselves in the market and taking advantage of market reactions to political, economic, and other investment events.

That said, attempting to make profit from short-term investments is just as likely to lose you money and add to frustration, as it is to grow your money. Investing in shares hoping to reap a quick reward is something that relies on lightning-fast decision-making, high-level computer hardware, a vast quantity of capital, and more than a little bit of luck. If you're looking for a short-term investment to keep your money safe from inflation, you're far better off looking at more stable investments, like certificates of deposit, savings accounts, and bonds. These instruments have a far more predictable value and can be used to more easily trade liquidity for security.

Long-term investment, though, is less about timing the market and more about time in the market. Long-term investment in income-generating investment tools takes advantage of the power of compound interest to generate wealth. According to the noted physicist Albert Einstein, compound interest is the most powerful force in the Universe. While that may be hyperbolic, the effect on your wealth generation should not be underestimated. Let's take a look at another example.

If you take $10,000 dollars and invest it at 3% yearly, which is a very modest rate of interest, at the end of the first year, you'll have $10,300. The second year, you'd earn interest on both your principle, so you'd get another $300, but you'd also earn interest on your previous interest, giving you $10,609. After 10 years, you'd have $13,439. After 20 years, you'd have $18,061. After 30 years, you'd have $24,273. Your money would more than double over that time without your having added anything to it.

If your goals are long-term and you have the capital on hand, the question of when to start isn't one you should be asking. The answer is now. Time in the market will, over the long term, do more to grow your wealth than waiting for interest rates to fluctuate slightly higher. You need to find instruments which produce a rate of return which will help you meet your goals, and which have a level of risk you can tolerate.

How much should I invest?

The answer to this question depends both on your goals and on your cash flow. If your goals are long term, it may be helpful to put a little bit away at a time to achieve those goals. This is a particularly helpful rule if you don't have a great deal of liquid capital on hand.

Investing small sums in shares can be a useful part of a broader investment strategy. Shares, more than other investment instruments, generally have a low threshold for investment. Many managed supers have high minimum investments required, which can price a lot of investors out of them as an instrument. Shares, on the other hand, can be bought individually, for a price that varies widely, from as little as a $.01 to as much as a few hundred dollars.

As I've said before, be careful of so-called "penny stocks"- called that because they cost very little. While it is true that investing $100 in those shares could see big returns, those stocks are valued at the price they are for a reason. Always take the company behind the shares into account, and consider all available options. If penny stocks were a good deal, they would be worth a lot more. No matter what you buy, you get what you pay for.

The answer to how much you should invest, though, depends largely on what you can afford. To figure this out, you need to determine your "cash flow"- or the amount of excess money you take in for a given period. If your income is $2000 per month, and the total of all your expenses is $1800 per month, then you have a positive cash flow of

$200. You may not want to invest all of that money, as you may wish to keep some in easier-to-access forms to make emergency purchases or deal with unexpected expenses. So you should invest that portion of your cash flow which will help you achieve your financial goals without compromising your near-term financial integrity.

How should I invest?

You have two options for how to invest in shares: direct investment or indirect investment. Quite simply, the difference between the two methods is the level of direct involvement you have in managing your investments. Direct investments involve you purchasing shares yourself or through a superfund or SMSF (self-managed superfund). Indirect investment involves purchasing shares of cash management trusts, property trusts, or managed share investment funds, among other instruments. Each approach has advantages and disadvantages.

Indirect investment likely places a few hurdles between you and investing. These types of instruments usually have minimum investment levels, and may require considerable notice before buying or selling to prevent speculative investment. These investments usually also have significant overhead costs. A professional manager is responsible for maintaining the fund and monitoring its investments, and that person will have to be paid a salary.

On the other hand, having a professional manager to follow the ups and downs of the market and seek a consistent return is a benefit in and of itself. This person is a professional who likely has both education and experience in managing the investment fund. They also invest as a full-time job, and so devote a great deal of attention to managing the fund. These kinds of investments also make investing far simpler. You have to make one decision: which investment instrument will you buy and for how much? The fund manager does the rest of the wealth management for you.

Direct investment, by contrast, requires you to do considerably more research. You are responsible for making all of the decisions about the management of your share portfolio. This can create quite a bit more stress in your financial life. You will have to continually work to provide returns to give you the rate of growth you need to meet your financial goals.

The benefits of direct investment are essentially the opposite of the disadvantages of indirect investment. You have far greater choice and flexibility. The only minimum you will have to meet is the minimum price to buy individual shares. You can choose when to sell and when to buy. You control the rate of return you will achieve by buying and selling shares.

The overhead costs for this kind of investment are also lower. You are managing your investments on your own time, and so the need for a professional fund manager to draw a salary from your return is far lower. You will usually have to pay a brokerage fee or commission per trade; shopping around at various purchasing locations can help keep these costs as low as possible.

When should I sell?

This is a far more complicated question than when to buy. Let's look at a few easy answers first. You should sell a share position when:

- You need the liquidity to meet your financial goals

- The company you invested in has changed in a way you find unacceptable

Those are really the only absolute times when sale is necessary. Otherwise, you're making a share sale based on whether or not you expect the return offered by the company to continue to meet your financial needs.

Bear in mind that selling shares isn't an all-or-nothing proposition. You can sell just part of a position if you feel that you need to rebalance your portfolio. You might do this if a stock has grown rapidly and unexpectedly as a way of controlling risk.

You might also see an imbalance in your portfolio as a need to increase your total investment positions. If you want to ensure that no one company comprises more than 10% of your portfolio, and one of them has grown beyond it, rather than selling those shares, consider this an opportune moment to invest in other shares. Maintain the balance in your portfolio that you expect to help you meet your financial goals.

You might also see this as an opportunity to reinvest the proceeds of your rebalancing. Perhaps you sell off a number of shares, anticipating the price to return to a lower level.

At that time, you might reinvest the money you made from predicting that price drop into the same original company. It is likely to continue to produce the same historical returns.

Most importantly, do not sell shares impulsively. Remember, time in the market is more important than timing the market. For your long-term financial needs, stability is the most important marker of success. Keep to your strategy, and focus on your goals. Not everything called a "better investment opportunity" is one!

In this chapter, we've gone over the basics of making a strong financial plan. We've focused on your goals, found out an ideal time to start, talked about how much and how you should invest, and about the perils of leaving a shares position too early. Knowing what you now know about your financial plan, take a moment and write down a few goals that you have for your financial future. In the next chapter, we'll look at a few different instruments you might use to achieve those goals.

Rising Markets

Technical analysis charts depict formations that can be used to determine movements in the market. The rising or ascending wedge is a chart pattern that shows a popular formation. For investors who use technical analysis, rising wedges can help to identify a stock pattern that is coming to a high point and will soon turn down.

As traders, you can use the rising wedge to your advantage to beat the market. But be warned that if they are not used correctly, the pattern will lead to further losses for you.

The traditional wedge pattern used by technical analysis consists of two upward sloping trend lines. The closing highs are connected by the upper trends and the closing lows are connected by the lower rising trend. The higher highs and lower lows pattern tends to take place at an interim top in the market or stock. During the ascending wedge formation, volume is likely to decline. Ascending wedges can occur on charts with any time frame. It can take a while to completely form when used in daily, weekly or monthly charts. The figure below shows a 60-minute chart with a rising wedge formation.

When the market is looking bleak, promising prospects can often be found in latent opportunities. This occurrence is strongly recognized in the Chinese culture. In their language, crisis and opportunity share the same character.

Panic within the Shanghai stock market resulted in opportunities throughout the financial markets worldwide in February 2007. What looked like a crisis at first because of a sharp downfall and percentage lost over several days, actually turned into abundant opportunities.

Let us take a look at what occurred. First, we'll revisit the rising wedge, which is often seen in bear markets. This type of pattern occurs in charts when the price rises with pivot highs and lows which converge toward a sole point called the apex. One trend line is used to draw across at least two pivot highs and another connects at least two pivot lows. Using these two trend lines, a convergence will be seen. The pattern has the resemblance of a bear flag (shown in the figure below).

© 2006 IQ Chart www.swingtracker.com

When the big drop in the market began in February 2007 as a result of panic in the Shanghai stock market, the market continued to move downward until it reached the bottom in March of the same year. Afterwards, the market generally began to recover over a period of several days. Many technical analysts recognized the futures pattern as a rising wedge (or bear flag).

When a rising wedge is being formed, there are a few indicators that you can look out for to determine whether the pattern you are seeing is real or false. A true rising wedge normally moves to the right, the volume should be reducing and a divergence between price and volume should be shown. In addition, analysts will examine how far the retrace has advanced since the start of the downward trend. If there has been advancement in the move too much over the 50% Fibonacci level, the pattern being observed may not be valid. However, if it is under that 50% level, validity of the pattern prevails.

A trader will tend to be fond of this pattern because the target is reached very quickly after the breakdown occurs. With other patterns, a confirmation must be shown before the taking of a trade. However, most times wedges do not need confirmations; they usually break and fall quickly to their targets. The start of the upper trend line or the fist pivot high located where the trend line is connected is normally the location of the targets.

The figure below illustrates the short entry which was made when the price broke through the lower trend line (786.0) at the closing of the bar that broke through the trend line. It took several days for the formation of the pattern before the breakdown. However, it only took six hours to hit the target.

© 2006 IQ Chart: www.swingtracker.com

The ratio of risk to reward for rising wedges is very low, which is why it is a favorite for professional patterns. But there exist many false patterns disguised as rising wedges. The only way to distinguish between a true rising wedge and false one is by calculating the price/volume divergence, making sure the failure is within the 50% Fibonacci retrace level.

In summary, the rising wedge is a good indication of a high point that will soon start turning down. Due to the many false wedges that may present themselves, it is very important to properly identify the pattern before taking any action based on the charts.

Falling Markets

Another formation within technical analysis charts that can be used by traders is the falling wedge. This type of pattern can generally be described as bullish and signals the likelihood of a price break upwards through the wedge and into an uptrend.

The falling wedge is identified by a convergence of the pattern's trend lines, where both slant downward because the price is being traded in a downtrend.

With falling (or bullish) wedges, the pattern slants downward (see figure below) and away from the existing bullish trend.

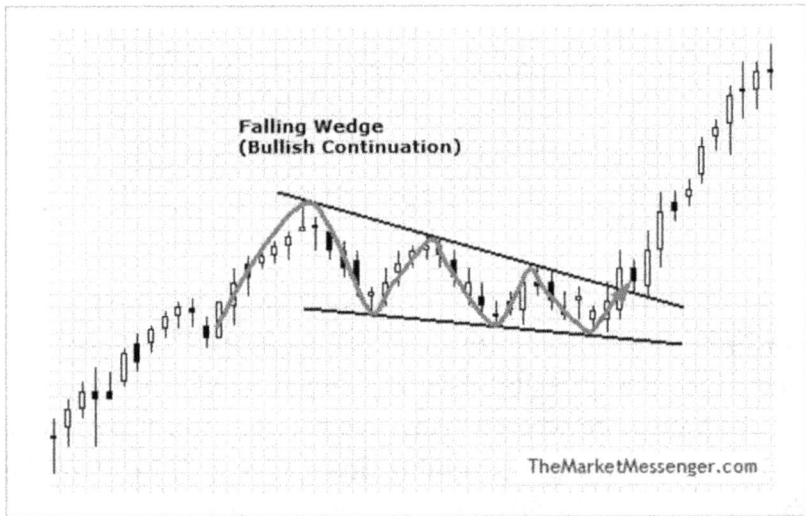

Within the boundaries of the wedge, prices will continuously have lower highs and lower lows.

While a wedge is forming, levels of volume normally reduce. In order to ensure that the pattern does not fail, a sharp rise in activity should occur concurrent to the breakout. Falling wedges that are successful will often result in sharp rallies over a short time period. They may sometimes be hard to recognize at first, but they can be very useful when correctly observed.

There are varying views on how targets should be set for a bullish wedge. While some traders believe that a full retracement of the lost ground during the wedge formation should be expected, other trades project the preceding move's size from the point of breakout in order to set a relevant target.

A wedge is normally shown as a continuation pattern that slants against the existing trend. However, on occasion, a wedge can appear at the end of a trend and represent a reversal pattern. When it is shown as a reversal, the slant will be in the direction of the trend.

Irrespective of whether the wedge shows during the trend or at the end of a trend, when analyzing you should be aware that slant of a true wedge is always opposite to that of the trend following the breakout.

The signal to buy is formed when the price actually breaks through the upper resistance line.

As you can see from the figure above, the downwards slant of the upper resistance line is of a steeper slope than the line of the lower slope. Thus, we can confirm that pattern as one of a falling wedge.

The figure above also shows that, based on what was happening in early April, the two converging trend lines represent the boundaries of the price traded until the breakout point (5.30). Unlike the normal types of breakout, there was little increase in trading activity. The point at which trading volume increased was only evident when the main target (6.50) was broken. Within two months, the pattern has included the stock's replication of the $3 move and the stock was trading for as much as 9.00

On the other hand, the figure below shows a falling wedge reversal.

The stock was in the middle of an intermediate downward trend, which saw a fall between June and September/October from 45 to 36. When that period came to a close, trading of the price began with a couple of downward-sloping (as well as converging) trend lines. The pattern had similarities to a wedge, but like most wedges, it was slanted in the prevailing trend's direction (and not against it).

The figure above illustrates that volume generally reduced as price was being traded within the pattern. This occurrence is typical during the formation of a wedge. Then, in the middle of October, following a surge of trading activity, the price broke out above the reducing resistance line and started a new upward trend.

Only two weeks following the breakout, the stock has risen by almost 15% to 41. This example is one of a falling wedge reversal pattern that is quite rare.

As with the rising wedge, the ability to identify the falling wedge can be an advantage to you as a trader. Practice will make perfect so get practicing to be able to identify these formations easily and without error!

What to Trade

There are a baffling number of investment instruments available. Each of these instruments has associated risk and reward values, and choosing the right one can be really difficult. This chapter will provide a broad overview of the kinds of financial instruments you can invest in, and how each compares in terms of convenience, risk, and potential for growth.

Always keep your plan in mind. Just because a particular investment instrument seems like the hot new trend doesn't mean it's right for you. You need to make these decisions with the long-term in mind, and that means making a strategy and sticking to it.

In this chapter, we'll look at shares, futures contracts, options, warrants, exchange-traded products (like managed supers), CFD's, REIT's, interest rate securities, and credit-linked notes. There's a lot of terminology to consider, but don't be intimidated. It's just a name given to a collection of instruments which have similar risks and rates of return.

Shares

We've already talked a lot about shares. Shares are probably what most people think of when they think about investing. Shares are little pieces of a company. When you purchase shares, you buy a small percentage of a company. If that company does well, the value of the share will increase. If that company does poorly, the value of the share will decrease. That's pretty straight forward.

It gets a little more complicated when discussing kinds of shares. There are a few kinds of shares that need specific attention in your strategy-building. These are income shares, blue chip shares, growth shares, cyclical shares, and defensive shares.

Income shares are just shares in particular companies that have historically paid larger than average dividends. These may be investment companies which accrue large gains using the capital borrowed from shareholders. They may just be big companies that are unlikely to grow dramatically, and so use dividends as a way to attract investment. If you're investing over the long term, the residual income from income shares can be a nice way to passively grow your wealth. They're unlikely to generate much in the way of capital gains, or appreciation in share price, but are also less likely to lose value.

Blue chip shares are shares in companies which have been around a while and are fairly large. General Electric, Proctor and Gamble, and Wal-Mart would be examples of blue chip shares. Shares in these companies are a specific kind of income share. They're very unlikely to lose much value, because they provide something which is subject to fairly inelastic demand, but they're also unlikely to gain much. These companies are already huge, and so their stock price won't change much if they grow by 1-2%.

However, these shares have provided historically higher-than-average dividends, paid regularly and steadily. This fact makes this class of shares a very safe place to invest for long-term growth or income.

Growth shares, by contrast, are shares in companies experiencing growth at a faster rate than other companies in their industry. These shares tend to increase in value faster than industry supers or other, more diversified instruments. Investing in these kinds of shares can be risky, though. The price will only continue to rise as long as investors believe the company will produce higher than average profits for its industry.

These shares can be the best way to build wealth over the short-term, but they involve a considerable amount of risk. They can very easily lose value or under-perform compared to their industry. While making investment decisions in growth shares using the latest news and the most reliable information makes it possible to minimize the risk of this loss. Remember - even professionals who invest in growth shares are wrong some of the time.

These shares can also be exposed to high levels of volatility. Minor changes in the market can trigger broad sell-offs of a stock, and most investors follow the lead of big, well-funded super managers. When someone in one of these positions decides that a growth share is exposed to too much risk, and that they should sell it from their investment portfolio, many other investors follow suit. The resulting large sell-off can destroy the value of the stock and hinder your efforts to build a financial future.

These shares also do not usually offer dividends or residual income sources, as they use all of their earnings to fuel new growth. The only way to make money from investing in a growth share is to properly time both entrance into and exit from the market. This requires diligent planning, careful attention, and a great deal of knowledge and effort to execute successfully. Still, it is a high-risk, high-reward option for investors who need to meet short-term goals.

Cyclical shares are shares in an industry which is subject to general economic trends. Capital manufacturing is an example of an industry which has predominantly cyclical shares. As the economy grows, new businesses open up, using available, cheap credit. These companies need to buy new equipment to grow and expand, and so the share price of companies which make that new equipment is likely to increase as their profitability increases.

However, when the growth of the economy slows and credit becomes more expensive, demand for the products these companies produce is likely to level off, causing the growth in these shares' prices to slow and perhaps decrease. Investment in these shares is usually done over the short-term: a period of around a year.

Because cyclical shares tend to respond more to broader economic indicators, like interest rates, GDP, new housing development, and so on, investment in cyclical shares tends to be somewhat safer than trying to pick winners in growth shares. The gains are usually somewhat less extreme, though, as the owners of these companies have experience in managing responses to big economic trends, and so slow the valuation of their stock in order to promote steady, sustainable growth.

The opposite of cyclical shares are defensive shares. These shares are in industries which are relatively insulated from larger economic trends. An example would be biopharmaceuticals. The demand for prescription medication, for instance, is relatively inelastic, meaning it does not fluctuate greatly in response to price changes. Regardless of the condition of the larger economy, people will likely demand the same amount of antibiotics and cholesterol medication, and a change in price does not fundamentally affect the price of shares in companies which manufacture these products.

These shares can be used to hedge against the market fluctuations which attend cyclical shares. While it is difficult to get much in the way of growth out of shares in these industries, they still reflect an important part of a well-balanced portfolio. They can serve as a risk management strategy, as they will experience some growth, particularly relative to cyclical shares, in more difficult economic times. These positions make a good counterbalance to riskier investments in cyclical or growth shares.

Futures Contracts

Futures contracts are agreements to buy or sell something for a fixed price at some point in the future. For example, ABC Corp is currently valued at $1.00 per share. You think the price is going to go up, so you initiate a futures contract to buy into ABC Corp at $1.50 per share. You will usually have to pay a fee for this contract, but then you have agreed to buy a fixed number of ABC Corp shares at $1.50 per share. If the price of ABC Corp stock increases to $5.00 per share, then your right to purchase those shares at $1.50 reflects a considerable gain. You could buy ABC Corp shares at a significantly discounted rate (close out the position) or you can sell the option to someone else who would like to buy those shares.

In either case, you make money from the difference between the value of the share or other financial instrument when you close the option and the value you agreed to pay for it. Futures contracts can be purchased on a wide variety of financial instruments, from shares to shares in supers to commodities like oranges or cattle. In each case, the futures contract is a form of speculation. You are essentially betting on the behavior of the market. If you're right, you can make considerable capital gain. If you're wrong, you're out the difference between your futures price and the current value.

Futures contracts are fairly complicated financial instruments, and their chief role in your portfolio should be to mitigate risk. If, for example, you are heavily invested in ABC Corp, you might initiate a futures contract on ABC Corp's biggest competitor, expecting that if the value of ABC Corp drops dramatically, the price of their competitors would rise. Because you purchased a futures contract in advance of the ABC Corp share price falling, your futures contract is more valuable. In this way, you mitigate the risk involved with being too heavily invested in a single company.

Options

Options are a form of futures contract with a slight modification. Initiating options contracts provides the buyer the right, but not the obligation, to buy or sell shares or commodities at a given price. There are two kinds of options: call options and put options. Call options govern the purchasing of shares. Put options govern the sale of shares.

Gains from option contracts occur in much the same way as gains from futures contracts do, and they serve a similar purpose in your portfolio. Call and put options are usually more expensive, but they also reflect less risk. If the option is unattractive at the time it comes due, you are under no obligation to exercise it.

Let's return to ABC Corp for an example. If you are heavily invested in ABC Corp, you might invest in a put option to hedge against a drop in price. Let's say the price of an ABC Corp share is $5.00, and you purchase a put option for $4.50. If the price of ABC Corp drops to $3.00, then your put option saves you $1.50 per share. If the price of ABC Corp holds steady, then you would, presumably, not exercise the option, and be out the cost of the option contract. The cost you paid for the option contract would reflect the cost of mitigating your risk.

Options and futures are often called "derivatives," because their value is *derived* from the price of other financial instruments. As an individual investor, be wary of these derivatives. They are complex instruments that are most often used by large firms to counterbalance dangerous investments.

Successfully maintaining derivative options in your portfolio will require constant attention and intervention, and are unlikely to contribute to your long-term financial stability.

Positions

Another aspect of trading to learn is when to add positions. Surprisingly, in practice many traders are afraid to add to a winning position, but they do not hesitate to add to a losing position. Let us clarify what a successful trader needs to do with relation to adding positions.

When you are experiencing a losing position, adding to this will only maximize the loss. Instead, you are to add to positions that immediately go in the anticipated direction. In this way, you are maximizing your profits. Similarly, with losing positions, you are not to add to them and increase your losses.

Consider making reservations at a restaurant that you dislike because the food poisoned you and the staff was unbearably rude. This probably describes an untenable situation for you. However, by adding to a losing position, you are essentially requesting more of what you dislike in the same way.

Further, when eating at a restaurant that you love because the food is wonderful and the staff is great, would you decide to leave early because the experience is too good? By failing to add to a winning position, you are missing out on possible profits.

Pyramiding is a highly aggressive and risky strategy to undertake, which is appropriate for full-time professional traders who have the ability to control risks and are disciplined enough to implement a trading plan consistently. It involves adding to positions as movements in the price follow the desired trend direction.

In this way, pyramiding allows for an increase in profit if the trend continues in the direction that is desired. However, pyramiding will also increase losses if the trend changes direction. As a result, an essential element of pyramiding is risk control.

With regard to the tradeoffs between risk and reward, it will quickly turn against the trader using a pyramiding strategy when the price trend reverses. Due to the fact that adding positions changes the total cost of the whole position toward the last price on a per-unit basis, a quick change in direction to the initial entry price can lead to a huge loss. In cases where the price reversal occurs quickly and steeply, e.g. on a gap or fast market, it can be nearly impossible to limit risk as planned.

Previously specified price points that confirm the direction of the trend will trigger the signal to add positions. The predetermined price points may be based on bands of volatility, moving averages, logical points on a chart, trend-lines and resistance levels penetration among other things.

There are four types of pyramids that can be used in a trading strategy. These types include the standard (or scaled-down or upright), inverted (or equal amounts), reflecting and maximum-leverage pyramids.

The standard pyramid begins with a large original position and then additions which are predetermined. These predetermined additions systematically decrease in size according to the price movements in the indicated direction of the trend. For instance, an initial entry is for 200 shares, the price moves up to the next predetermined level and 100 more shares are added, upon reaching the next level 50 more are added, then 26 more, for a grand total of 376 shares.

Increments of equal share-size are added to an original position with the inverted pyramid. This type of pyramid is best explained by example. Following an initial entry for 200 shares, 200 more are added as the price reaches the next predetermined level. As the price increases, positions of 200 more are added, then an additional 200, for a total of 800. In this case, the average cost per share is a lot higher so that a price reversal of a smaller size takes away all profit. There is greater potential for reward from the inverted pyramid. However, the reward is at the cost of much higher risk in comparison to the standard pyramid.

The reflecting pyramid involves the systematic addition to a position up to a previously specified price level. The position is then reduced systematically as the trend continues. In this way, the reflecting pyramid is not purely a trend-following method. If the price moves in a big way in the indicated direction of the trend, the reflecting pyramid would lead to smaller profit when compared to the standard and inverted pyramids.

With the maximum-leverage pyramid, maximum size is continuously added up to the accumulated profit limit and margin requirements. This strategy is the most aggressive one available and it offers the greatest potential for reward, as well as the greatest potential for risk and the worst ratios of reward / risk. To avoid ruin altogether, the maximum-leverage premium should be used in conjunction with tight exit rules.

Adding positions can also be discussed in the context of money management. Profit gains can be increased by addition positions to winners. Traders could include in their trading plan that positions should be added when the gain is 50% of the targeted profit. In this way, the trader is letting the profits run. In addition, there should be a strictly defined stop loss to ensure that losses are cut quickly.

The number of positions held at any one point in time can be increased as your account size grows. However, it is not necessary to have too many positions.

Renowned investment visionary Warren Buffet has been known to say that diversification is simply an excuse for laziness. Traders should always remember that it is not necessary to over-diversify or to have over a dozen positions. This belief is contrary to those commonly held by most investors.

It is true that these rules may not apply to very large accounts of over a million dollars, but even accounts of this size can benefit tremendously from maximizing the gains of profitable trades alongside rules for money management.

You will be surprised by how much your profits will increase if you simply add to winning trades and refrain from giving in to your emotions and adding to losing positions.

Warrants

Warrants are a type of derivative that are managed by a bank or another financial institution. Their underlying value is based on some financial instrument in which the bank has invested, like an exchange-traded fund, a share, a price index, a commodity, or a currency. These instruments give the holder the right to purchase these financial instruments from the person who issued the warrant at a specified price and time.

For example, if XYZ Bank were to issue warrants for ABC Corp shares at $3.00, they would charge some fee for that contract, and, in exchange for that fee, you would have the right to purchase shares of ABC Corp Bank at $3.00 per share. If the price of ABC Corp shares were higher than $3.00, XYZ Bank would have to purchase shares of ABC Corp at market value and sell them to you at a loss, resulting in a gain for you. If the price of ABC Corp shares were lower than $3.00, then, depending on the warrant contract, you would either be obligated to purchase those shares at a higher price, or you would be out the cost of the warrant contract.

Warrants are frequently issued by banks and other financial institutions to mitigate their risk. This does not make them inherently bad investments, but it should encourage you to exercise caution in purchasing them. Banks, particularly large ones, did not get large by losing money. The best use for these instruments for individual investors is as a hedge against their own risk.

Exchange-traded products

Exchange-traded products are supers which seek to achieve some pre-established financial outcome. They may try to maintain a price which reflects some index, or they may seek to own small quantities of shares from many different companies within an industry. Exchange-traded products are good ways to establish a diverse portfolio easily, and a professional manager will work to maintain the balance of the portfolio on your behalf.

These products enable you to trade more broadly in industries than in individual securities. As such, the price of exchange-traded products tends to be somewhat more stable than the price of individual shares. These tools can be an excellent addition to your portfolio given their diversity, versatility, and general resiliency.

When choosing an exchange-traded product, look for ones with low management fees. These fees reflect the quantity of the investment which leaves the fund to pay for the various costs of administration, including the salary of the manager and the upkeep of the manager's office. While a high management fee should not be a deal breaker, remember that those fees reflect a portion of your investment which you will not see.

Contracts for Difference (CFD's)

Contracts for difference are leveraged instruments in which a seller agrees to pay the difference between the current value of an asset and its value at the time of contract execution. If the difference is negative, the buyer instead pays the seller. These are complicated speculative instruments which rely on market fluctuations to achieve their value.

If P buys a CFD from Q for ABC Corp while the price of ABC Corp is $1.00 per share, and at the time of contract execution the price of ABC Corp is $2.00 per share, Q has to pay P $1.00. If, on the other hand, the price of ABC Corp dropped to $.50 per share, then P has to pay Q $.50.

The advantage of CFD's is that they enable an investor to gain exposure to a wide variety of financial instruments for a small initial investment. The downside is that they are incredibly risky and can expose investors to significant losses. They derive their value from market fluctuation, and so are very difficult to predict.

Real Estate Investment Trusts (REIT's)

Real estate investment trusts are portfolio investments in a wide variety of real estate. An REIT might purchase a few dozen square kilometers of land in an economically desirable area, then make money from the sale of that land. REITs may also buy pieces of mortgages on properties. These instruments are usually professionally managed. They may or may not pay interest or dividends, and their level of risk is usually determined by the professional manager.

Interest rate securities

These are securities that pay some consistent interest rate or dividend over their lifetime. An investor makes an initial investment and then receives constant payouts from that investment at a regular interval described in the initial purchase contract. These regular payments persist over the life of the instrument. Think of them like a reverse credit card. You make an initial investment (the credit limit of the instrument), and the person who borrows the money pays interest on the loan until they pay off the loan in its entirety. Examples of interest rate securities are corporate bonds and Australian Government bonds.

These kinds of investments are generally fairly low risk, as unless the issuing institution loses all its money, you are likely to be paid back. Purchasing bonds can be a good way to add slow growth and income generation to your portfolio. These instruments provide a measure of security and a calculable rate of return on investment.

Credit-linked notes

These are loan certificates created through a Special Purpose Company (SPC) or a trust. The organization offers as collateral on the loan AAA-rated securities. Investors purchase parts of this loan from the organization, and, in return, are paid a regular or adjustable rate of interest during the life of the loan. When the loan comes due, or reaches maturation, investors receive their initial investment back, unless the AAA-rated securities that were collateral for the loan default or go bankrupt. In this case, investors would get back a percentage of their investment, called the recovery rate.

There are many different financial instruments to choose from. Carefully consider the risks and rewards of each and each one's suitability to achieving your long-term financial goals. Remember, many of these investment tools are built in such a way as to obscure how they are making money. Always exercise caution when investing, and avoid any deal that sounds too good to be true. These instruments are all either loans or bets, so evaluate them like you would if someone on the street wanted a loan or to wager with you. Consider the odds of return versus the risk, and invest wisely.

Increasing Returns without Leverage

The concepts of leverage and margin are particularly common within the foreign exchange market. There are several definitions of leverage to be found from various sources and they include:

- "The mechanical power or advantage gained through using a lever."

- "The degree to which an investor or business is utilizing borrowed money."

- "The use of credit or borrowed funds to improve one's speculative capacity and increase the rate of return from an investment, as in buying securities on margin."

Therefore, leverage can be thought of as the ability to utilize the funds at your disposal to increase the amount that you can borrow from an external party. The capital that you have for the transaction is called the margin.

For instance, when you want to purchase a house but do not have the cash to pay for all of it up front, the bank will look at your salary and determine whether you are able to afford monthly installments. The institution is allowing you to leverage your salary and you can borrow the funds you require to purchase the house. The concepts of margin and leverage have a similar meaning in the foreign exchange market.

Making high returns is possible without the use of leverage. The best way to explain how this can be done is by example. The following story shows how even a trader with terrible timing can make good returns without leverage.

Market guru Jim Rogers made a famous short trade in gold. In 1980, gold experienced record highs alongside rising inflation and geopolitical unrest. Rogers knew that the rise in gold could not continue indefinitely, but he was too early to the trade. The price of gold continued to rise to $800 per ounce, but he shorted out at around $675. Unlike most traders, Rogers was able to hold on and profit. He eventually covered the short at almost $400 per ounce.

How was Rogers able to succeed? Well, he certainly used no leverage in his trade. Rogers did not employ a margin, so he was never at the mercy of the market and was able to liquidate his position whenever he decided to do so instead of having a margin call force him out of a trade. By not using leverage on his position, Rogers was able to do more than merely stay in the trade. He was able to add to it at higher levels and ended up with a blended price that was better overall.

By using no leverage at all, Rogers gave himself a much bigger margin for error. As a result, there was no need for him to be correct to every cent to be able to secure huge gains.

A reason why many traders are drawn to the foreign exchange market is the availability of very high leverage. Therefore, large positions can be held with a small amount of money. If there is a movement in the market in the direction of the trade, gains are multiplied by the amount of leverage used. A lot of traders find this attractive.

But foreign exchange trading using leverage can be likened to driving a car. Everyone who has driving experience is aware that when a car is driven very fast, it becomes more difficult to control. For instance, if you are driving at a relatively slow speed and accidentally make a turn of the steering wheel, the car may move slightly but will also allow you to rectify your mistake and move back into position. However, if you are driving relatively fast and make the same mistake with the steering wheel, the consequences could be extremely serious and even fatal. The direction of the car will change completely and you may not have the precious seconds necessary to amend the position of the car and avoid a collision.

When trading in foreign exchange, leverage equates to high driving speed. The more leverage you are using, the faster the speed at which you are driving. It follows, then, that the smallest change in the market can result in irreparable damage to your trading account. On the other hand, if you drive slowly and cautiously you may take a little bit longer to get to your destination, but you will reach it unharmed.

By trading with little or no leverage, a trader may make a smaller profit but no single trade will completely close your trading account. You will have the opportunity to remedy the situation afterwards with another trade.

However, large amounts of leverage increase the risk of ruin of a trader's career or, at the very least, drain a trader's account. Trading systems that are reliant on excessive margins often fail following one or more losing trades.

A major characteristic of the foreign exchange market is its volatile nature. Using leverage simply increases the already high level of volatility and thereby significantly heightens the levels of your overall risk.

An important point to remember about trading without leverage is that you can only lose all of your money if that currency loses all of its value. Most currencies, e.g. the United States dollar or the Euro, will always have some value, so trading without leverage is a safe way to go.

Leverage will cause a trader to lose focus and ignore market developments and instead concentrate on volatility and the developments in your account. However, by trading with no leverage, you can easily review and assess your accomplishments knowing that they are based on your trading strategy and not leverage. Utilizing high amounts of leverage, in addition to draining your personal account, can remove your common sense and logic when trading.

Let us take a look at how leverage can drain your capital. Using simple calculations, a $4,000 expense will result if a trader makes 40 trades per month at a 20:1 leverage and a 5 pip spread. This expense is present before you even lose a single trade. Now, let us apply this amount to a trader that loses approximately 35% of his trades. This percentage represents a good performance, but even with this successful track record, the trader will be losing 14% of his account.

This trading scenario is very optimistic. But, even so, after a long period of time an excellent trader will break even but most traders will end up with losses. Traders may not start losing right away, but they will feel the hurt in the long-term. Leverage may offer the potential for gains, but it will also slowly empty your trading account.

Many individual traders believe that trading with little or no leverage is not "sexy". But institutional traders often do not use leverage when trading foreign exchange or the amount used is very small. It could be argued that the returns generated by traders working for institutions in this market are small. However, the results may be minimal because institutional traders have less leeway. Individual traders have greater freedom to tailor their margin to suit their style of trading and tolerance for risk.

I cannot stipulate what the best margin is for traders. You may have to use simple trial and error. However, at least in the beginning, it may be better to utilize a lower amount of leverage (or none at all).

You should ignore the fact that leverage is such a major buzzword in the foreign exchange market, and instead make your own evaluation. High leverage may not be best for you as a trader. However, the marketing teams of various brokers in the industry extensively promote high leverage. Why are they so interested in getting you to trade with high leverage? The answer is simply because the likelihood of you succeeding when trading with high amounts of leverage is very low. When it comes down to it, the brokers who make the market are the ones competing against you in trades and making money when you are losing.

The lesson to be learned from Rogers is that traders need to slowly enter into their positions using tiny amounts of capital and use very little leverage, or none at all, to enter trades. Even with poor timing, traders can still be profitable if they take small positions using little or no leverage so that the poorly timed trades can easily absorb any adverse actions on price.

Increasing Returns
with Leverage

We have looked at trading with little or no leverage. Now it is time to look at the other side of the coin. There are experienced traders who disagree with the approach of avoiding highly leveraged markets and only trading in cash-based markets.

The argument presented is that trading with leverage is not any more risky than trading without leverage. Furthermore, depending on the type of trading, the higher the amount of leverage used, the greater the risk is reduced.

Leveraging can assist investments but there is also an accompanying risk element attached. If a trader uses leverage to make an investment which moves against the trader's expected position, the loss will be much greater than if the investment had not been leveraged. Both gains and losses are multiplied as a result of leveraging.

The common belief is that using leverage is highly risky because it multiplies the potential profit or loss that can result from a trade. However, another view is that leverage makes extremely efficient use of trading capital. Traders value leverage because it affords them the opportunity to trade larger positions and they need less trading capital to do so.

Using leverage does not change the possible amount of profit or loss that can be made from a trade. Instead, it lessens the amount of trading capital required and therefore releases capital to be used for other trades.

For instance, a trader who wants to purchase 1,000 shares of stock at a price of $20 per share would perhaps only need $5,000 of trading capital. Therefore, the $15,000 remaining would be left for additional trades. Many professional traders view leverage in this way.

Apart from using trading capital efficiently, leverage can also significantly lessen the level of risk association with specific types of trades. By illustration, a trader who wants to invest in 1,000 shares of a particular stock at $10 per share would need cash of $10,000. All of this cash would be at risk.

However, if a trader wants to invest in the same particular stock that has the same profit or loss potential using a highly leveraged market, e.g. the warrants market, he/she will need only a small proportion of the cash of $10,000, perhaps $500, and only that amount would be at risk.

The argument here in simple terms is the more leverage the better. There are professional traders that will always seek to trade in high leverage markets instead of non-leveraged markets. They look at new traders who choose to avoid using leverage as amateurs.

Importantly, a trader's exposure to leveraged positions is not limited to the trade amount or the trading account balance. If your liability exceeds your trading balance, your broker may require further deposits to cover the stated margin requirement, otherwise known as a margin all.

Therefore, however you decide to use leverage when trading, it is essential that you ensure that your trading is kept within tight parameters that are affordable. In addition, steps should be taken to minimize your risk exposure as far as possible to avoid a leverage-induced catastrophe.

Even with the associated expense from financing costs of leveraged positions and higher commission costs per transaction, trading with leverage is still beneficial. By using leverage sparingly, it will amplify the profits of certain positions and effectively maximize trading profit potential.

Trading positions using leverage can often be unjustifiable, especially if they are rolling overnight and are continuous positions with a focus on the long-term.

Positions over the long-term with margined products may become overly burdensome if the costs of funding the leverage outweighs the profit potential to be gained. The longer a position is left open, the higher may be the applicable costs.

Traders need to know how to use leverage to capture higher returns. Pyramiding is an aggressive trading strategy which has the potential to lead to substantial profits. However, inverted pyramids carry too much risk to be utilized.

Pyramiding is a leverage trading strategy and refers to a trader adding to profitable positions in order to take advantage of an instrument's good performance by using margin from unrealized gains. As the position grows, pyramiding allows for substantial profits to be secured. However, a close eye needs to be kept on the market because pyramid trading will also increase losses when the trend reverses.

To recap, the standard pyramid begins with a large starting position which is followed by additions that are predetermined. These additions reduce systematically in size as the price moves in the trend direction indicated.

The inverted pyramid adds to an initial position in increments of equal size. The average cost per share works out to be much higher. The result is that a smaller reversal in price wipes out all profit. While the inverted pyramid offers greater levels of reward, it is at the cost of much higher risk when compared to the standard pyramid.

Risk can be minimized when using leverage while trading by setting tight stop losses. Remember, these are automatic orders to close losing positions once losses reach a certain point or trigger. The stops should be set at a limit that is a little below the recent lowest price point so that your position will reverse if your transaction value falls to a new low. It is important to have a stop in place to avoid runaway losses and allow you to concentrate on other areas of your portfolio without having to obsess about the possibility of devastating, out-of-control, leveraged losses.

When using leverage while trading, the strategy of pyramiding should be used by experienced traders to maximize profits. As the inverted pyramid has too high a risk to reward ratio, the standard pyramid should be consistently utilized.

Super and Shares: What's the connection?

With a strong financial plan that meets your goals in place, it's time to look at how to achieve them. Investing in shares for growth or dividends seems daunting- there's so much terminology to go over, and the time investment to create and maintain a balanced portfolio is significant. On the other hand, investing in supers seems like a dangerous loss of control. Someone else is in charge of managing your investments, and that person may not have your financial best interests at heart.

There is another option. You can create a self-managed super fund or SMSF. This is an increasingly popular option for people who want the security of diversification a super can offer, combined with the flexibility to control where and how your money is invested. With a do-it-yourself SMSF you can have the best of both worlds. You can customize an investment strategy to meet your goals with the "fix and forget" security of super investment.

There are three key reasons why an SMSF may be the right choice for your investment decisions: control, flexibility, and personal investment choice. These are three benefits you won't find with other financial instruments. Let's take a closer look at what each of these benefits are, how an SMSF can help you obtain them, and why you need them in making your investment decisions.

Personalized control over the direction of your investments is an obvious benefit of an SMSF. You get to decide the level of risk, the goals, and the level of diversification. You become responsible for ensuring your own financial future.

SMSF's offer this level of control because they allow you to determine what balance of shares comprise your super. Instead of picking from a preset range of share packages, you can customize your own to achieve exactly the balance of risk and return that meets your goals. Designing an SMSF like this takes work, but it is ultimately a rewarding endeavor.

Control over your own financial future is a big part of the reason to begin investing on your own in the first place. You want to be in charge of your own retirement, major purchases, charitable actions, and so on. An SMSF can be tailored by you to meet exactly those goals.

Flexibility is the ability to adjust on the fly. The future is uncertain. You may find yourself in a job you love and decide you want to do it forever. If you're locked in to a managed retirement fund, you may have difficulty changing the way your fund is managed to meet your new goals and financial needs. You may have to pay a significant penalty to cash in your managed super if you need the money for some other purpose.

An SMSF offers the flexibility you need. Because you set up and manage the fund, you set the rules. If your goals change, you can make modest adjustments to your investment strategy to meet your new goals.

Flexibility is an important part of achieving financial security. The ability to make your money meet your needs is a vital part of achieving financial independence. Managing your own super can help you find that level of flexibility to make your financial dreams come true.

Personal investment choice is the ability to make share purchase decisions according to your personal ethics, knowledge, and sensibility. If you think solar power is a great thing for the future, you can invest in solar power to further the cause. If you find alcohol consumption or cattle production immoral, you can avoid investing in shares of companies which engage in those practices. If, looking at the state of the economy, you think one specific capital goods firm is likely to charge ahead of the pack, you can choose shares in that company and take advantage of your insight.

An SMSF offers the opportunity to do exactly this. Because you're the financial manager, you get to pick the funds that meet your predictions and judgments about how the economy will or should function. You have the power to decide what a worthwhile investment looks like, and only you can figure out what to do with your money.

Personal investment choice gives you the chance to get some return from your hard work in making smart investment decisions. You can read every press release, product specification, and analyst in the world, make an informed decision, and see the rewards. You also have the power to vote

WINNING THE WEALTH GAME WITH SHARES

with your pocketbook and only endorse those companies, by buying shares in the ones that align with your personal values.

You might think that in order to obtain such benefits, you'd have to comply with complex regulations, deal with demanding audit requirements, and keep a mound of paperwork organized. Obtaining such service used to cost quite a bit. In order to make an SMSF worthwhile, you'd have to hire a top-notch accountant with experience in maintaining supers. These kinds of administrative costs would really undermine your return.

Today, though, competition in the SMSF service provider market has considerably lowered those costs. Because there are many companies competing to provide SMSF service to individual investors and technology has enabled significant automation of the more arduous parts of SMSF administration, that overhead continues to decline. This decline has made it possible for any investor, even those with only modest investment capital, to access diverse investment products.

There are a few requirements to be aware of in setting up your self-managed super fund. In addition to thinking about your investment goals, you need to watch out for a few simple regulatory hurdles. These are considerations to make before you invest your first dollar.

First, an SMSF can have no more than 5 members. This regulation is in place to stop every major investment firm from setting themselves up as an SMSF and avoiding stricter oversight that comes with professionally managed supers. Who should be a member? Everyone who makes a contribution is a trustee in the fund, and therefore a member. You and your spouse can share retirement savings. You might also include an eldest child who would have trustee rights. If you own a small business or corporation, you might find it beneficial to invest in an SMSF through your corporate entity.

Trustees are all required to prepare and implement an investment strategy. An investment strategy is aimed at the investments of the SMSF to achieve a desired outcome and a minimum level of performance. It is a plan for making, holding, and realizing the Fund's assets, consistent with the Investment Objective of the fund. This strategy should reflect the ideal level of growth, the acceptable level of risk, and the conditions under which buying and selling of shares will occur. When making your investment plan, think back to your goals. If you are investing over the short term, your investment strategy will probably reflect a more aggressive, high-growth, high-risk approach to your investing. If you are investing over the long-term, your investment strategy might reflect a more defensive, diversified, income- or dividend-oriented approach.

In creating your investment strategy, it's vital to focus on your goals. Don't think of the investment strategy as a strait jacket which confines your investment decisions. Think of it like a company mission statement. Your investment strategy is there to help you guide your decision-making process and keep you oriented to achieving your financial goals. You're not taking charge of your SMSF because keeping track of various investment tools is fun. You're doing this to achieve some goal with your money. Keep yourself focused on that principle and make your investment strategy accordingly.

The fund trustees are tasked with ensuring that investment decisions made by the super are done in accordance with their investment strategies. Under the Superannuation Industry (Supervision) Act 1993 ("SIS Act") the Trustee of the SMSF is solely responsible and directly accountable for the management of the members' benefits.

The trustee has a duty to make, carry out and document decisions about investing the assets of the fund and to carefully monitor their performance. This duty involves formulating and implementing an investment strategy. This important duty is prescribed in the SIS Act as a covenant (an obligation of the trustee).

The investment strategy must have regard to the whole of the circumstances of the Super Fund, including the following four items.

1. First, the risk involved in making, holding and realizing the SMSF's investments, and the likely return from these investments, having regard to the SMSF's objectives and its expected cash flow requirements.

2. Second, the composition of the SMSF's investments as a whole, including the extent to which the investments are diverse or involve the entity being exposed to risks from insufficient diversification.

3. Third, the liquidity of the entity's investments having regard to its expected cash flow requirements, for

example: payment of tax, superannuation surcharge liability of the members, lump sum benefits if a member leaves the SMSF, or regular pension payments;

4. Fourth, the ability of the SMSF to discharge its existing and prospective liabilities.

The purpose of this obligation is to protect the members' retirement benefits, to minimize the risk of irresponsible or incompetent investments, and to ensure investments are made in accordance with the sole purpose and investment provisions of the SIS Act.

Under this approach to managing the investments, the Trustee should implement a due diligence process promoting well thought-out and responsible decision making. This also protects the Trustee from action by members if the investments turn out to be disastrous.

The establishment of and adherence to a written investment strategy is required by the law, which enables the creation of SMSF's. If you don't create a valid investment strategy, or if the decisions made in maintenance of the investments violate the investment strategy, the ATO, (the regulatory agency which oversees investment instruments), may find your SMSF non-complying. Talk to a financial planner, lawyer, or other trusted investment adviser to ensure your investment strategy follows the letter of the law.

The investment strategy must also satisfy all of the fund members. It must be able to genuinely reflect the purpose of the fund, which is the reason why the trustees invested money.

It must also include guidelines for maximizing member returns without exposing members to long-term risk. It must deal with a long-term diversification goal, and must provide full benefits for all members as they reach retirement age.

The regulatory burdens facing you as a potential SMSF manager aren't inconsiderable, but they are manageable. So long as you and your fellow trustees are honest and unambiguous in discussing and documenting your financial goals and you consult with a financial expert, your SMSF can help you make the most of your money.

Robotic Trading

By this point, you may be thinking that utilizing an automated electronic trading platform could be the best way to go about managing your funds. A system like the Cooltrade software does have the capacity to manage your shares, and only requires you to first set up a goal or strategy.

Before you become too set on using this method, it would be very valuable to step back and look at the details of how this actually works, and whether or not this tool is a proper fit for you.

For the purposes of this section, when talking about robotic trading software usable by the general public we will continue referring to the Cooltrade platform, one of the superior automated trading systems available to the public. Although there are other possibilities available, Cooltrade provides you access to tried and tested starting strategies that were created by numerous Computer Scientists, professional Day Traders, and stock gurus. The Cooltrade system is also one of the only complete trading systems that doesn't require complicated programming knowledge or experience to use. This way you won't need to enroll in your local neighborhood advanced algorithms class to get a quality strategy up and running. All of the programming has been completed by the tech pros, so you only need to run the software.

Cooltrade Fully Automated Stock Trader

So what does software like this actually do that you can't do yourself? The short answer is that it thinks like a computer. Cooltrade connects from your personal computer to data feeds using your internet connection. Every minute, Cooltrade performs multiple scans through the current stock information available, and uses this information to decide which new stocks should be invested in and, if it is appropriate, when to sell your current holdings. The sale of your current holdings could be based on protection needs, if the software thinks the current stock is going to fall too far for comfort, or on a major profit goal. If the stock has reached its projected peak, Cooltrade initiates an automatic sale to reap the benefits of the peak before the stock can drop too far. This way Cooltrade maximizes profits, while protecting and maximizing your hard earned savings.

The Truth of Today's Market

The amount of automated trading that happens on today's market is unbelievably high. In complementary fashion, the amount of activity from buy and hold traders is shrinking at an increasing rate. This may sound obvious (holding stock is the point of the buy and hold strategy after all), but keep in mind that this is in comparison to historically tracked numbers.

In 2012 Morgan Stanley reported that over 84% of the market is now controlled by High-Frequency Trading Software. A quick internet search on how long the average shares are held reports that the majority of shares actively traded on the market are held for only 22 seconds at a time. Large companies are literally making tons of profit by shifting a huge amount of money into a stock, holding it while it rises by a penny or two, and then selling and repeating.

With this kind of current market environment, understanding the process and thought behind High-Frequency Trading is becoming more and more necessary.

By understanding the basic rules of share pricing we can conceptualize how High Frequency trading works. Some stock in question is selling at a stable reasonable price, so the "thought process" behind the program, its trading algorithms, decides that the time is right to purchase.

The software then proceeds to purchase a large volume of the shares, driving up the price of the stock. Other High-Frequency Trading Programs may see the sudden increase, and also buy a large quantity of shares driving the prices up even higher. Once satisfied with its profit, our initial software will sell all of the shares it has, earning pennies for each share. The stock begins to dip, and other programs will sell their shares, hoping to save any profit they currently have or prevent any losses.

Due to the nature of this competition, High-Frequency Traders constantly try to improve their computing capacity, or find new ways to process their orders faster. It is not uncommon for these types of companies to try to buy out the fastest servers at the largest and fastest nodes of broadband connection throughout any country they currently reside in.

Eliminating computing limitations, the processing time for such activities is approaching the limits of how fast data can travel through fiberglass or the air, which is not quite the speed of light, but fast enough to seem instantaneous to any human competitor.

This incredible speed, the nature of today's technology-driven market, is what makes personal trading software such as Cooltrade so important. In another few years, software such as Cooltrade may become a mainstream way for the average person to trade on the stock market, as trading continues occurring faster and in larger volumes with the increases of future technological speed capabilities.

Pros and Cons of Robotic Trading

While Cooltrade does seem like an impossibly useful product, as with everything in life, there are distinct pros and cons. Any decision to place your own savings in 'the hands' of a robot should come with a deeply honest discussion of the good and bad that can come about because of this.

Let's first go over the potential negative effects or setbacks that could arise from using a robotic trading platform. You'll notice that a majority of negative impacts come simply from the nature of the product, and the fact that it is a computerized process.

And we'll also take a close look at the potential positive effects you'll see from utilizing this software. The benefits range from peace of mind, to security from sudden drops, to potential for making a great deal more profit than using the traditional buy and hold method allows.

Cons

1. There is a Lack of Human Contact you may get with a Personal Stockbroker

Interacting with your computer can be a confusing task for some, and daily email usage alone can be a frustrating experience. If you choose to use a computer program to manage your funds, but are uncomfortable with daily computer use, you may feel very insecure about letting your funds manage themselves without your interactions and input.

When you use Cooltrade, you must be comfortable leaving the computer to do its work. If you constantly tweak rules and "over-optimize" it will become increasingly likely your funds could be impacted in a negative way.

You will also notice that you will not have a direct access to your friendly human finance guy when trusting a robotic service to handle your shares. A real, live person can be a very calming thing for some people; knowing there is a fellow human watching your back simply has a psychologically calming effect for most people. Despite a computer's seemingly infinite capacity for speedy calculations, computers just aren't capable of having a human touch.

2. You Require an Internet Connection During the Trading Day

Due to the nature of Cooltrade, it requires the ability to check on current stock positions multiple times a minute. It is recommended that you utilize a broadband connection while using Cooltrade.

Some rural locations around the world do not have access to high speed internet yet, simply because the broadband connection lines have not been established. There are some alternatives that could help hit this requirement, such as satellite internet, but this can be influenced by inclement weather, solar activity, and a great many other natural (and unpredictable) phenomena.

It is important to note that a slower internet connection would not completely disable you from utilizing Cooltrade, but could cause the program to run in a less-than-optimal way.

3. You Require Basic Computer Troubleshooting Skills

While Cooltrade is a simple set up and let loose type of software, anyone who has used a computer knows that computers can be the most finicky devices about certain seemingly simple things.

It's easy to forget that computers are constantly performing ridiculously complex operations throughout their active life. Although you may only have your internet browser open, a multitude of services and programs that are managing your computer are active in the background and you will never see or hear from them. These include encryption and decryption of your internet connection, the rendering of graphics on your screen, inputs from your mouse, keyboard, writing and reading from memory, screening of background code for malicious software. This is just a short list of basic processes, and every one of these constantly competes for time to perform calculations within your CPU.

You will need to be able to check on your computer and ensure that connections are working properly throughout the day. Going back to the Flash Crash story, if your Cooltrade software loses connection prior to an event like that, it is rendered unable to respond to the current events. This could in turn lead to potential losses on your holdings, and losses on profits that could have been made as the market recovers.

Pros

1. Cooltrade Offers Fantastic Customer Support

All of those technologically based cons are known by the team behind the Cooltrade software, so they have professional trainers and support people to help you make the most of the software. Using a program complex enough to require over five million lines of code comes with a learning curve. The Cooltrade team has created informational videos and articles to teach you how to use the software, and if that doesn't help, they offer prompt and courteous phone support for anyone who may need it.

The Cooltrade team makes their support a point of pride for the software, and claim to offer hours of personal phone support on any topic related to the software. As long as you have a computer and internet, there should be no reason for you to worry about understanding and being able to use the system.

2. Automatic Research and Stock Selection

Cooltrade automatically does all of the legwork for you, several times every minute. Once you have selected a strategy to use, the software will automatically seek out and track changes in stocks for changes that fit your desired strategy. This way, you don't actually need to know very much about the stocks you are investing in; selections happen autonomously.

This drastically cuts down on time you are required to spend on managing your funds by doing your own research. It also allows you to begin creating a profit while you are still learning the rules of the game.

Cooltrade can also diversify your stock holdings based on your desired goals.

3. Cooltrade Significantly Reduces Mental Stress

Letting the software do your legwork is nice, and lets you relax a bit. Knowing that millions of lines of logic, checks, and professional insight are all at work protecting your savings is really an impressive weight lifted from your shoulders. Cooltrade offers an advantage over human monitoring in this area. A human managing your funds may miss important details that the software checks multiple times a minute. A computer never needs a cup of coffee to get started in the morning, so you have excellent monitoring from the opening to the closing of the trading day.

Letting the software do its job, you have the same ability the huge multi-billion dollar companies and banks have - near instantaneous ability to shift and react to the slightest sign that things are changing, as soon as it happens.

4. Cooltrade Provides a Space to Safely Test Your Ideas

Most programs and professionals look to the past to examine strategy. Cooltrade takes a more active approach, and monitors your ideas using current market data. Rather than using data that may very well never repeat itself, Cooltrade takes in active information that can give a far more accurate estimate on how your strategies will perform on the current market.

This take on strategy testing is a unique one, and one that Cooltrade performs very well. Market conditions are rapidly changing, and based on seemingly infinite variables as previously mentioned.

Looking at the past may provide a quicker view of how your strategies would have fared, but that method will never prepare you for current events, especially related to current political opinions. What may be a thriving and profitable business chain one day could be a political battlefield the next based only on a single social media post. These days, as society adjusts to an ever increasing internet social media presence for everyone, past events just aren't enough to gamble your shares on. A forward-looking, slow and thoughtful approach is a newer idea, but one that has worked very well for users of the Cooltrade platform.

Statistics on the Cooltrade Software

Let's now take a look at the advantages you can gain from using Cooltrade versus utilizing a buy and hold strategy. According to Morgan Stanley 84% of all stock trades are done by high-frequency computers. Did you know the average trading volume is now over 6 billion shares every day? In today's computer driven market the average stock is held for just 22 seconds! Automated traders take unfair advantage of buy and hold investors. Institutions take billions in profit by constantly trading millions of shares moving only by pennies. The game has changed and so should you.

Total AUD assets in managed funds in 2012 were $3 trillion dollars. The Dow Jones total 5 year return from March 28, 2008 – March 28, 2013 was 13.72%, or an average of only 2.74% annually. Many managed fund managers can't sell when the market falls because of forced redemption rules. They're stuck! Yet managed funds still rake in billions in fees whether the market is up or down.

Comparing Strategies: Buy & Hold vs. Cooltrade

Compare actively trading 100 shares VS Buy and Hold -

Example strategy for simulating over a 3 year period.

- On May 3rd, 2010 Microsoft stock price was $30.86.

- On August 12th, 2013 Microsoft stock price was $32.87.

MSFT	Trades	Profit
Buy & Hold	1	$ 200
Cool Trade	62	$ 4,500

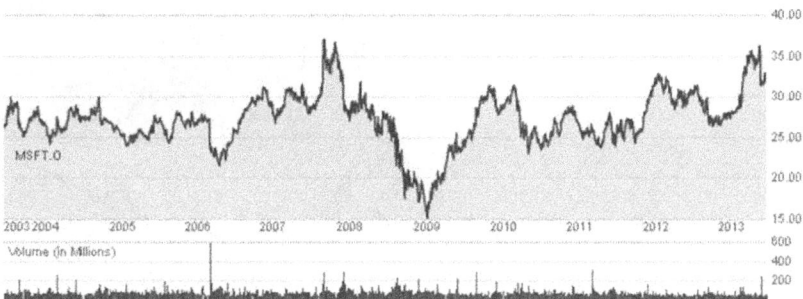

- On May 3rd, 2010 JP Morgan stock price $43.53.

- On August 12th, 2013 JP Morgan stock price $53.09

JPM	Trades	Profit
Buy & Hold	1	$ 1,056
Cool Trade	129	$ 11,400

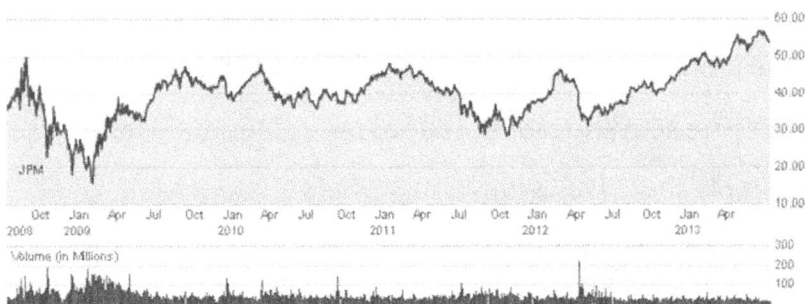

- On May 3rd, 2010 Halliburton stock price $31.39

- On August 12th, 2013 Halliburton stock price $46.02

HAL	Trades	Profit
Buy & Hold	1	$1,463
Cool Trade	186	$ 13,725

CoolTrade harnesses the power of robotic trading software to continually look for profits and execute trades. The program monitors up to 8,000 stocks simultaneously, executes your trades fully unattended and is easy to set up to harvest and protect your profits.

Useful Links

http://www.asx.com.au/education/shares-education.htm - Education center provided by the Australian Stock Exchange

AnalystsEdge.com - A news aggregator and community for financial information.

BullPoo.com - A community that lets you trade information with others via blogs and discussion.

Covestor.com - Show off your trading skills, track others, even earn fees from allowing people to follow your trades after you've proven yourself.

FeelingBullish.com - A social network for investors with analysis and blogs.

PredictWallStreet.com - Use charts, news, and information to help make predictions in this community.

SocialPicks.com - A social community for investors to trade tips and track performance.

SteamStreet.com - Track your portfolio, get investing ideas and discuss them with others.

StockFiend.com - A social network for people looking to learn about stocks, share tips, and make friends.

TheUpDown.com - A social network for investors to share information and try to form well thought out investing strategies.

Wikinancial.com - A virtual stock market site for you to test your strategies and compare them with others.

CakeFinancial.com - Watch the portfolios and real-time trades of top investors, friends, family, and learn from them.

ChartSetups.com - Offers analysis on stocks, day trading, investing, stock charts and more

ETrade.com - Offers lots of tools to help you maximize your portfolio.

GStock.com - Using architecture similar to the Seti@Home program, GStock leverages the unused computing power out there in the world to project stocks for up to 10 years.

Investools.com - Offers courses in trading and investing.

Marketocracy.com - A site that attempts to find the best investors in the world and let you track what they do so you can follow along and learn.

MarketSimplified.com - A centralized site for charting, portfolios, risk assessment and more.

MyTrade.com - A source for all your financial news and is fully customizable.

Schwab.com - Get advice from one of the largest financial service providers in the country.

SeekingAlpha.com - Brings together investment advice from blogs, money managers, and investment newsletters.

SmallCapDirectory.com - Search over 18,000 small cap and micro-cap stocks.

StockCloud.net - See which companies release the most press releases in a tag cloud like setting.

TippingMonkey.com - Learn how to do trades and play the stock market while only risking virtual money.

Special Offer

Would you like to find out if an automated share trading platform is the right vehicle for your situation?

Book in right now for your FREE consultation, your bonus for reading this book.

To Grab Your Bonus Session go to

http://www.winningthewealthgame.com.au/sharesbookoffer

Not all share strategies are created equal. We will share more information on how automated systems can save you time and make money. Look forward to speaking to you soon.

Other Books in the Series

Winning The Wealth Game In Business

Winning The Wealth Game With Property

Winning The Wealth Game by Protecting Your Assets

Winning the Wealth Game by Creating Multiple Streams of Income

Winning the Wealth Game Online

Winning the Wealth Game in Network Marketing